# Essentials of General Management in Africa

This concise overview of the practice and processes of management in the African context is the first of its kind, and the introductory volume in the new *Essentials of Business and Management in Africa* short-form textbook series.

This book covers the activities that all managers undertake regardless of their functional specialisation and is organised around a model of management that consists of planning, organising, staffing, directing and controlling. After introducing each topic, the authors discuss particular characteristics of Africa and African countries and how these influence the topic being covered; for example, relative levels of poverty, prevalence of small and informal businesses and the inadequacy of infrastructure will influence aspects of planning and decision-making, and motivation. Each chapter includes illustrative real-life examples and experiential exercises/short cases. The book begins with a general overview of the African continent and ends with discussions of ethical issues and corporate social responsibility including the management philosophy of Ubuntu.

Undergraduate and postgraduate students in Africa and other parts of the world with an interest in the area will appreciate the focus on a region so little discussed in the business and management literature. Due to this dearth of material, this book will also appeal to current and future practicing managers in African countries.

**Lemayon Lemilia Melyoki**, Senior Lecturer at the University of Dar es Salaam Business School, Dar es Salaam, Tanzania.

**Betty Jane Punnett**, Professor Emerita at the University of the West Indies, Cave Hill, Barbados.

**Essentials of Business and Management in Africa**
Series Editors: Bella Galperin, Betty Jane Punnett, Terri
Lituchy, and Ali Taleb

This series of shortform textbooks offers a range of books which focus on the essentials of various aspects of business and management in the African context.

In focusing on the core elements of each sub-discipline, the books provide a useful alternative or supplement to traditional textbooks, and can be used by trainers and managers as well. Each book provides information on basic concepts in the sub-discipline and examples to illustrate how these concepts are affected by the African context.

**Essentials of General Management in Africa**
*Lemayon Lemilia Melyoki and Betty Jane Punnett*

For more information about this series, please visit: www.routledge.com/ Essentials-of-Business-and-Management-in-Africa/book-series/EBMA

# Essentials of General Management in Africa

Lemayon Lemilia Melyoki and Betty Jane Punnett

Routledge
Taylor & Francis Group

NEW YORK AND LONDON

First published 2021
by Routledge
605 Third Avenue, New York, NY 10158

and by Routledge
2 Park Square, Milton Park, Abingdon, Oxon, OX14 4RN

*Routledge is an imprint of the Taylor & Francis Group, an informa business*

© 2021 Taylor & Francis

*Library of Congress Cataloging-in-Publication Data*
A catalog record for this book has been requested

ISBN: 978-0-367-43519-6 (hbk)
ISBN: 978-0-367-86179-7 (pbk)
ISBN: 978-1-003-01751-6 (ebk)

DOI: 10.4324/9781003017516

Typeset in Times New Roman
by Apex CoVantage, LLC

# Contents

# About the Authors

**Dr. Lemayon Lemilia Melyoki**: Senior Lecturer at the University of Dar es Salaam (UDSM) Business School; he has researched and published numerous journal articles in peer-reviewed journals and several book chapters in published research volumes in fields of entrepreneurship, leadership and management, and corporate governance.

**Prof. Betty Jane Punnett**: Professor Emerita, University of the West Indies. Her research focuses on culture and management, particularly in Africa/ Caribbean. She has published widely in international journals, several books (recently, Managing in Developing Countries, International Perspectives on OB) and book chapters.

# 1  The African Continent

## Chapter Summary

This chapter provides a contextual background for the remaining chapters dealing with aspects of management. We give an overview of Africa's current levels of development and consider African countries' role in today's global business environment. We briefly look at Africa's geography and present a short history of Africa highlighting developments over the past 600 years. Measures of development for African countries' performance are discussed. Throughout we relate issues to doing business and managing in the African context. Students of management and managers need this background picture to understand effective management in the African context.

---

### Learning Outcomes

After completing this chapter, you will be able to:

- Discuss the implications of Africa's geography for doing business.
- Give an overview of African cultural values.
- Explain the recent history of the African continent.
- Explain how slavery and colonialism have influenced African countries.
- Discuss changes over the past 30 years that influenced business in Africa today.
- Discuss the current situation in Africa including issues associated with trade and foreign investment.
- Review African countries' performance on various development measures.
- Relate the information in the chapter to managing in Africa today.

The origin of the word 'Africa' is debatable. Some believe the name referred to native Libyans, ancestors of modern Berbers. Others believed

---

DOI: 10.4324/9781003017516-1

that it was named by Epher, a grandson of Abraham, whose descendants claimed to have invaded Libya. Several other accounts exist.

There are many stories today of entrepreneurs making fortunes by catering to the needs of Africa's rural poor. One African entrepreneur set up a company using solar power to show videos and make ice cream. The company's vans travel to rural villages with no electricity, and although the people have little money, they save up to attend these events.

An anthropologist proposed a game to a group of African children—he placed a basket of sweets near a tree and had the children stand 100 m away. Then he announced that whoever reached the basket first would get all the sweets in the basket. He said 'ready, set, go!' To his surprise they all held hands, ran together towards the tree, divided the sweets equally among themselves and all enjoyed them. He asked them why and they answered 'Ubuntu' by which they meant 'How can one be happy when the others are sad?' Ubuntu has been translated as 'I am because we are' and provides a strong and positive message for all.

In the past, Africa was portrayed as having poor governance, poverty, economic stagnation and social services lagging the rest of the world. African countries were considered difficult for businesses, with many regulations, slow procedures, substantial corruption and needing illegal payments to get things done. Infrastructure was poor with unpaved roads, inefficient ports, poor banking systems and so on, making setting up and managing a business challenging and seemingly impossible for some. Today, this is changing. Concerns remain across Africa, but progress has been made. Several countries are performing well on development indicators. Income/capita is generally growing; more people are getting out of poverty and have more disposable incomes for goods/services. More people are better educated so the stock of skilled labour is increasing. We discuss development in Africa, then African geography and history and measures of development.

## Africa's Development: An Overview

A combination of factors contributes to socioeconomic changes in Africa. Importantly for managers, African countries are implementing reforms to improve economic management, liberalise economies and improve resource utilisation. These reforms create opportunities for businesses and encourage the flow of foreign direct investments (FDIs) into the continent. Tanzania enacted reforms to attract FDIs through incentives to entrepreneurs/investors, including institutional mechanisms for promoting investments. Other African countries have made similar efforts.

Africa's abundance of natural resources, especially extractive ones, has attracted new investments in the past 20 years, especially from the People's Republic of China (PRC). The increasing presence of Chinese business is encouraging others to re-examine the perceptions about Africa. The concept of the 'fortune at the bottom of the pyramid' (Prahalad, 2006), illustrating the potential of the world's poor as a market, has also encouraged businesses to consider African markets.

'Africa' means different things to different people. For some, images of animals migrating and safaris to see lions, elephants, giraffes, rhinos etc. For some, thoughts of child soldiers, famine, poverty and war. For others, feelings of reverence for the birthplace of mankind. All are part of the picture of Africa, but for businesspeople today, *Africa* means opportunity. *Africa*, especially now, is 'open for business'. The term 'African lions' has been used to refer to successes of countries and businesses and points to Africa's potential. There are substantial numbers of businesses that see Africa as the next big growth frontier and Africa has been described as in the midst of a historic acceleration, lifting millions of people out of poverty, creating an emerging consumer class and propelling growth in many economies (Kaberuka, 2010).

The world, however, is constantly changing. In 2019–2020, the world was affected by a pandemic (COVID-19). The results are expected to be devastating for world economies and individual countries. We do not know the outcome for Africa, but forecasts suggest a substantial decline in gross domestic product (GDP)/capita and FDI, although some sources suggest continued growth in Africa at relatively high rates.

Africa contains many and varied countries and to manage effectively requires understanding its geography, culture and history. Next, we briefly describe Africa's geography, dominant cultural values and review historical development. These topics are complex, and we provide a superficial overview. Readers should pursue these topics to get a more well-rounded perspective. In addition, historians and others do not always agree on the reality of the situation in Africa, and the interested reader may find alternative explanations. Our attempt is to provide 'a bird's eye view'.

## Geography, Cultural Values and History

Firstly, we describe the African continent from a physical perspective. We consider the size and makeup of the continent.

### *Geography*

Africa is the second largest continent in the world (Asia, the largest), measuring over 11.5 million square miles (over 30 million km$^2$), with a population of over a billion. The Economist's (2010) map of Africa illustrates its size, with China, India, Japan, Mexico, the United States and Western Europe fitting into the continent together. The continent covers 20.4% of the Earth's total land area.

Africa encompasses more than 50 countries. Various sources identify 54, 56, 57 countries and Answers Africa (2020) cautions it is not clear which territories can be considered countries. World Population Review (2019) says 54 countries, 9 territories and 2 independent states (with limited/recognition) are widely used estimates and, given Africa's complex political situation and colonial legacy, the exact makeup and number of officially recognised countries are contentious. We can say there are many, they are varied and most people agree on 54. Africa is often divided into regions—north, south, west, east, central and sub-Saharan (countries south of the Saharan desert, distinguished from the rest of Africa). There are economic groupings recognised by the Africa Union (AU) mirroring these: Arab Maghreb Union (AMU), Southern Africa Development Community (SADC), Economic Community of West African States (ECOWAS), East Africa Community (EAC), Economic Community of Central African States (ECCAS) and Common Market for Eastern and Southern African States (COMESA).

African countries range from very large, for example Algeria with about 7% of the continent's land mass, to small island countries, for example the Seychelles, 115 islands along the eastern coast. Egypt belongs to the AU, although a small part of Egypt is in Asia, and it is often grouped with Middle East countries. The continent has many tribes/ethnic groups, with some very large and others small. The Democratic Republic of Congo (DRC) has about 200 tribes/ethnic groups and Tanzania has some 120. The largest tribes/ethnic groups are the Fulani and Yoruba. All tribes/ethnic groups have their own languages and cultures. The current make-up of the continent in terms of countries is the direct result of colonialism. The map in Figure 1.1 shows the continent and its countries.

This map illustrates the variation in the size and shape of countries; some small, others large; some with lengthy coastlines, others landlocked with no ports. Africa's topography is varied, including high mountains (Kilimanjaro, Tanzania at about 6,000 m), flat plains (the Rift Valley), the world's longest river (the Nile, running from Burundi to Egypt into the Mediterranean) and the deepest (the Congo). It has some of the largest animal sanctuaries in the world, including Selous Game Reserve, Serengeti National Park, Ngorongoro Crater, Central Kalahari Game reserve, Masai Mara and Kruger.

Across the vast continent, cultures vary and cultural characteristics are important for doing business. Next, we look briefly at cultural values identified in the African context.

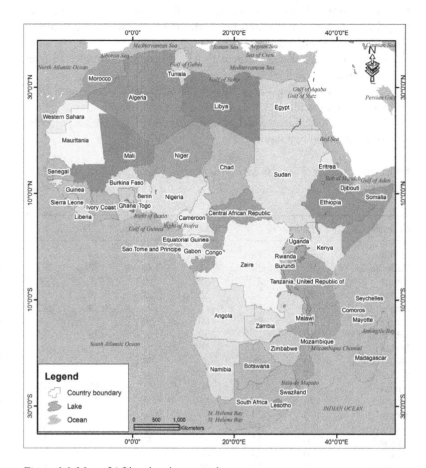

*Figure 1.1* Map of Africa showing countries

## Cultural Values

African people appear to share certain cultural values, based on the Hofstede culture value model. Hofstede's model is Western-designed but has been used worldwide. It was not intended to capture African-centric values; nevertheless, scores provide a comparison of African countries with other countries. The values measured are:

- Power distance—degree to which differences in power are considered right and acceptable.
- Individualism/collectivism—degree to which individual/group activities are stressed.

- Masculinity—degree to which traditional masculine values (assertiveness, achievement, material possessions) predominate over feminine values (nurturing, quality of life).
- Uncertainty avoidance—degree to which certainty is preferred over uncertainty/risk.
- Confucian dynamism—degree to which society takes a long-term view, focusing on the future.
- Indulgence—degree to which gratification and enjoyment are preferred to restraint and regulation.

Following are scores for 16 African countries (with the United States for comparison):

| Country | PDI | IDV | MAS | UAI | CD | IND |
| --- | --- | --- | --- | --- | --- | --- |
| Burkino Faso | 70 | 15 | 50 | 55 | 27 | |
| Cabo Verde | 75 | 20 | 15 | 40 | 12 | 83 |
| Egypt | 70 | 25 | 45 | 80 | 7 | 4 |
| Ethiopia | 70 | 20 | 65 | 55 | 7 | |
| Ghana | 70 | 15 | 40 | 65 | 4 | 72 |
| Kenya | 70 | 25 | 60 | 50 | 7 | |
| Libya | 80 | 38 | 52 | 68 | 23 | 34 |
| Malawi | 70 | 30 | 40 | 50 | | |
| Mozambique | 85 | 15 | 38 | 44 | 11 | 80 |
| Namibia | 65 | 30 | 40 | 45 | 35 | |
| Nigeria | 80 | 50 | 60 | 55 | 13 | 84 |
| Senegal | 70 | 25 | 45 | 55 | 25 | |
| Sierra Leone | 70 | 20 | 40 | 50 | | |
| South Africa | 49 | 65 | 63 | 49 | 34 | 38 |
| Tanzania | 70 | 25 | 40 | 50 | 34 | 38 |
| Zambia | 60 | 35 | 40 | 50 | 30 | 42 |
| Average | 71 | 28 | 46 | 53 | 19 | 51 |
| SD | 8.6 | 13.5 | 13 | 9.9 | 11.6 | 28.6 |
| *USA* | *40* | *91* | *62* | *46* | *26* | *68* |

PDI = power distance; IDV = individualism; MAS = masculinity; UAI = uncertainty avoidance; CD = Confucian dynamism; IND = indulgence; scores are out of 100.

Adapted from www.geert-hofstede.com.

Some cells are empty because these variables were not measured in those countries.

A review of cultural studies, using a variety of models, included 23 African countries, concluded that, in general, African countries were high on power differentials, collective and communal, moderate to high on uncertainty avoidance, somewhat masculine and short term in orientation (Punnett et al., 2019). One project looked for Africa-centric values, using

Hofstede, and found distinctive items related to CD, termed 'Traditional Wisdom' including 'wisdom is more important than knowledge' and 'wisdom comes from experience and time, not from education'. The LEAD project identified 'spirituality', 'belonging' and 'communal' as relevant in the African context. A limited number of countries have been studied. Even in the review only 23 countries out of 54 were included.

Next, information on Africa's more recent history. Africa is often called the birthplace of humankind, on the evidence that humans originated in Africa and migrated to the rest of the world. Africa's history is thus that of humankind and the following should be considered in that context.

## Brief History 1400–Present

History helps explain the development of any country and many features of today's African continent result from past events influencing development. History encourages appreciation of current management practices and provides a basis for improvements of organisational performance. Here we review three important historical periods, over about 600 years: the slave trade era (1400–1880s), the colonial era (1880s–1960s) and the post-colonial era (1960s to the present).

Early Africans lived in small communities and engaged in fruit gathering, animal keeping and limited agriculture. Communities were organised with emperors, kings or elders as leaders. Community leaders presided at traditional ceremonies and preserved traditional ways, values, customs and rules and behaviour. Differences existed between groups in terms of dress, housing, religious practices and so on. When groups experienced competition and conflict, it was for political power or economic advantage, not due to 'tribal differences', a term later created by colonial authorities.

### *Slave Trade Era*

The slave trade goes back well before 1400. Chami et al. (2002) noted accounts in the Greco-Roman period (1472 BCE) of East African contacts with Egypt and Persia for trade including slaves; and East African slaves in the Middle East in the ninth century organised their own army and revolted against the government in Baghdad. Early contacts occurred between Africa and Europe around the third century BCE when the Romans attacked Carthage (modern Tunisia). The Roman empire declined by the fifth century and European Barbarians took control of Western regions of North Africa. Romans again took control of North Africa in the sixth century but were driven out in the seventh century by the Muslim Arab invasion. Europeans lost interest in Africa until Portuguese mariners in the fifteenth century.

Prince Harry of Portugal conquered the kingdom of Morocco in 1415 and diverted the gold trade to Portugal. His exploration of the Atlantic coast resulted in extending Portuguese activities to include Kongo, the Gold Coast (modern Ghana), Angola, Mozambique and Benin. Many were converted to Christianity including the King of Kongo, Alfonso I (Mbemba Nzinga), who declared Christianity a state religion. Other European nations followed the Portuguese—Spain, France, Britain, Germany and Belgium. This was the beginning of the major slave trade era.

The effect of the slave trade was loss of people, otherwise available to work to better the continent. The slave trade affected social relations and disrupted institutions. In the early phases, people sold into slavery were largely taken as prisoners of war. Later, slaves were captured during raids, often involving villages or communities invading others. This led to hostile relations between villages and created an insecure environment. Other methods of enslavement were kidnapping, seizure and trickery by relatives and friends and through local judicial processes; thus, individuals began to turn on one another even within their own community. This created a vicious cycle—to defend oneself required weapons, which could only be obtained from Europeans or slave merchants, and to trade for weapons one needed slaves, often obtained through local kidnappings and other forms of small-scale violence.

This insecurity, violence and warfare had detrimental impacts on the institutional, social and economic development of African societies. Heywood (2009) argues that the slave trade caused the deterioration of domestic legal institutions, the weakening of states and political and social fragmentation. Given the importance of institutions for economic development, the slave trade eroded the foundation on which African people could build economies.

Effective management practices did not evolve, and this has an impact today. For example, people of the same tribe/ethnic group may express solidarity because they relate to each other more easily and with greater trust than with others from different groups. This affects staffing choices, leadership effectiveness and so on and may result in an 'in-group/out-group' mentality. Lack of trust requires detailed mechanisms for compliance, which increases transaction costs, reducing trade and business activities. This may have contributed to African countries doing more business with the rest of the world than among themselves (although there are additional reasons such as colonial ties and poor infrastructure).

The slave trade ended formally in the eighteenth century (1772) when the English Supreme Court declared the trade illegal on British soil and all slaves free; however, it took longer (50 years) and greater effort to effectively end the trade. Slavery was lucrative and alternatives, introducing commercial crops including coffee, palm oil and cotton, took time to become profitable raw materials for European industries. Once the slave trade was abolished, it was replaced with colonialism, discussed next.

## *Colonial Era*

Colonialism results in the temporary or permanent domination of the coloniser's mindset over local people. Africa's colonisation was preceded by the struggle for control of the continent among European powers. Partitioning Africa by Europeans started in the 1860s and was completed by the early 1900s. By 1905, Western European governments claimed control of almost all of Africa (Liberia was settled by African–American former slaves). Britain and France had the largest holdings, but Germany, Spain, Italy, Belgium and Portugal had colonies, and Ethiopia was under Italian domination from 1936. The majority of Africa lost sovereignty and control over natural resources, and colonial powers signed treaties, and drew their own maps with boundaries for colonies, protectorates and 'free-trade' areas.

The effects of the slave trade were reinforced, and civil conflict resulted when tribes/ethnic groups were divided into more than one country, leading to ethnic-based discrimination. Partition shaped the tribal/ethnic composition of states when they became independent, leading to ethnic polarisation, fractionalisation and inequality. This influenced institutional and economic development, provision of public goods and ethnic conflicts. Tribal/ethnic division is one of the main legacies of colonialism and exacerbated the rivalries engendered by the slave trade.

These factors have contributed to in-group/out-group tendencies in workplaces, where managers may favour members of their own ethnic background. This can affect an organisation's ability to hire and develop the best staff, motivation and commitment to the organisation and foster allegiance to personal networks over the organisation. This also fuels corruption within organisations.

Other effects of colonisation include the creation of countries that are landlocked, inhibiting access to global markets, because the cost of access to seaports adds to overall costs, and logistical planning is especially important and complex. Some countries are tiny with few resources compared to others that are large with abundant resources. Some have peculiar shapes, limiting the reach of a state beyond its capital and weakening enforcement of laws, so businesses must plan carefully relative to the legal situation that affects operations.

These effects continue to impact the political, social, economic and cultural life of post-colonial societies, referred to as neo-colonialism. Former colonies are controlled by former colonisers through indirect means, such as foreign aid and loans, control of international financial institutions, interference in internal affairs of independent states and so on.

Colonialism introduced new concepts of owning and managing property, that is, property rights. Earlier, land was largely owned communally. Cultural values usually define these rights, but in Africa these rights were imposed on the basis of European culture. Property rights in individualistic cultures means property belongs to an individual. In collective cultures, this is more nuanced, and property is viewed as a family/clan's or tribe's. This can provide challenges for organisations; for example, organisational members may feel that, if the Head is from their tribe or family, they are entitled to similar privileges/benefits as the organisation provides the Head. Even those with a western education, emphasising an individualistic culture have difficulty in applying this because it does not fit the African context.

Africans were obliged to learn European languages, because Europeans saw colonisation as a 'civilising mission' and had special policies and cultural programs of 'assimilation'. It is not surprising to hear people today say, '*yule jamaa ana roho ya kizungu*' meaning, 'that fellow has a white man's attitude' suggesting a better or superior approach, such as having good time management skills.

The overall result was African societies lacking confidence to pursue and implement their own original ideas, beneficial for business. Managers need to create an environment that helps rebuild the confidence of African employees to innovate at work. This may include special training to decolonise African people, by illustrating the strengths of African approaches to business, management and social issues. African's merit-based management systems are an example.

---

The Masai have a saying that '*minjo oltoroboni engawo*' which means 'don't give a bowl to a careless man as he will kill the cow'. In the organisational context, it means managers should not appoint incompetent people to positions of power because they will mismanage the very organisation that is meant to serve them.

---

During colonial times, native chiefs were used as agents. These agents/chiefs were selected because of loyalty to European administrators rather than for traditional legitimacy or were 'invented chiefs' who promoted tribal differences. Agents/chiefs enforced forced labour policies, ensured compulsory crop cultivation, recruited labour, collected taxes and fulfilled other colonial state requirements. These practices had long-term effects and today African leaders may still behave as if they are the law and the people are their subjects. Other legacies include neo-patrimonialism, authoritarianism and clientelism (centralisation of power with favours granted in return for loyalty), neo-colonialism (continued western control and dominance), tribal/ethnic divisions (rivalry and an in-group/out-group mentality).

In many cases, indigenous people were considered subjects not citizens. Colonial laws often allowed the authorities to imprison African subjects without charge or trial. These laws, inherited at independence, are still used in some countries. The behaviour of agents/chiefs seems to have been inherited by some African leaders who use public power to deal with their people, especially dissidents. Colonial powers ran colonies as colonial property and some post-independent African rulers saw their states as an inheritance passed on by the colonisers. This attitude may extend to organisations where CEOs run organisations if they were their personal property, including using organisational resources for their individual benefit. There is a need to develop institutions that counter this and help create a stable environment for business.

### Post-Colonial Era and Recent Performance

By 1977, 54 African countries had become independent states. After independence, African countries pursued strategies to bring about social and economic development. Problems related to weak economic growth began in the 1960s, and by the 1970s some countries had either stagnated or declined. For example, GDP/capita in copper-rich Zambia and the DRC fell through the 1970s due to declining terms of trade in the world market for copper, a fall in demand for primary exports and slow growth in agriculture. Poor management of economies also contributed to the deterioration. In the 1980s, African countries implemented reforms to save their countries from economic collapse. These reforms began to pay off in the 1990s and are seen in more recent performance.

### Recent Economic Performance

Most commonly, economic and investment measures are used as indicators of performance. We discuss how the Africa continent has performed in recent years.

A 2018 listing of African countries' nominal GDP puts Nigeria as the largest economy, USD 447.013 billion, South Africa second at 349.299 and Egypt third at 303.0 billion. The smallest economies are Sao Tome and Principe at 0.477 billion, Comoros 0.726 billion and Guinea Bissau 1.538 billion. These numbers reflect factors including physical size, population, resources, investment and so on. GDP/capita is a better indicator of the level of wealth/poverty in a country, relating economic activity to population size. GDP/capita ranges from quite high (USD) 34,865 in Equatorial Guinea, 28,712 in the Seychelles, 21,628 in Mauritius, 19,266 in Gabon and 18,146 in Botswana, to very low—Central African Republic 681, DRC 785, Burundi 808 and Liberia 867. From a global perspective, even the counties highest in Africa are not at the top by world standards. Equatorial Guinea and the Seychelles (#1 and #2 in Africa) are #37 and #47 in world rankings.

Africa.com (accessed September 2, 2019) shows GDP growth estimated at 3.5% in 2018, about the same as in 2017, and up 1.4% from 2.1% in 2016.

East Africa led with growth estimated at 5.7% in 2018, followed by North Africa at 4.9%, West Africa was 3.3%, Central Africa 2.2% and Southern Africa 1.2%. Growth is projected to accelerate to 4% in 2019 and 4.1% in 2020. This is lower than China's and India's growth but is expected to be higher than other emerging/developing countries. Africa's growing economies provide opportunities for businesses. Increasing GDP/capita means most people have more money to spend; especially important in Africa, because growth is from a low initial standard—the poorest people have the means to buy basic necessities, many people became middle class and want to improve lifestyles; the rich can afford luxuries. The opportunities in Africa span a very wide spectrum, from providing access to battery recharging for the poor, through refrigerators, freezers, washers, dryers and the like for the middleclass, to designer clothes and expensive cars for the rich. Distribution of wealth varies across countries and affects these opportunities.

Developments in Africa, particularly economic growth, are being noticed globally. Kaberuka (2010), in a McKinsey Report, said Africa was among the fastest growing parts of the world between 2001 and 2008, with average growth of 5.6% a year, and businesses were interested in capturing the opportunities generated by this growth. Growth was partially stimulated by a commodity boom, but stable macroeconomic conditions and structural reforms, privatisation of state-owned enterprises and lower barriers to competition contributed to the impressive growth. Inward FDI increased substantially, more than tripling during the period, including inflows from Gulf countries, China and India.

This was prior to the Corona virus pandemic. Forecasts during the pandemic suggest a serious decline in economic activity, including trade and investment, in the years following the pandemic. Some estimates suggest that African countries will not be affected as badly as some other countries, particularly Europe and North America. Nevertheless, the pandemic is causing serious dislocations in economies around the world and will certainly have an impact on African countries, even if they fare relatively well. Discussions in this chapter must be interpreted in terms of these events as they unfold.

### *Investment Measures*

FDI into Africa rose from USD 2,846 million in 1990 to USD 50,041 in 2012 (United Nations Conference on Trade Development (UNCTAD, 2013). FDI in 2012 was 17 times greater than that in 1990. Investors see Africa as an attractive place to invest, and many African countries have been interested in attracting outside investment. While FDI globally fell 16% in 2014 from USD 1.47 trillion to USD 1.23 trillion, influenced by fragility in the world economy, policy uncertainty and geopolitical risks in some regions, Africa's FDI flows remained stable at USD 54 billion (www.weforum.org/agenda/2015/07/10-trends-on-foreign-investment-in-africa/). More recently, according to UNCTAD (2017), FDI flows to Africa fell by 3% from USD 61 billion in 2015 to USD 59 billion in 2016, with five countries (Angola, Egypt, Nigeria, Ghana and Ethiopia) accounting for 57% of the continent's total inflows (Africa accounts for 3.4% of total global FDI). The overall decline of FDI was attributed to weak commodity prices in the global market.

In the twenty-first century, outward FDI has been changing, from domination by developed countries to emerging economies/developing countries playing a growing part. UNCTAD (2013) found outward investment from developing economies reached a record level of USD 460 billion. Combined with USD 100 billion from transition economies, these outward flows accounted for about 40% of global FDI. African countries shared in this, although investments are relatively small. Between 1990 and 2008, Africa's outward investment rose from USD 650 million to USD 9,309 million. By 2016, outward FDI was USD 18.2 billion, mainly from Angola, South Africa, Nigeria, Morocco and Botswana. Some investments were originally from outside Africa and then moved within the continent to exploit profitable opportunities. For example, SABMiller, a South African conglomerate, a division of AB InBev (a Belgian company) invested in Tanzania Breweries. There are many other companies, originating outside Africa, which started in one African country and spread to others.

One reason for current interest in Africa is the PRC's growing investment. The PRC's need for resources to fuel its own growth has made Africa attractive and significant investments have been in mining, and in infrastructure, and recently manufacturing. The rest of the world has noted Chinese interest and is competing with the PRC. CNN reported Japan's private sector was to invest USD 20 billion over three years, starting in 2017. Prime Minister Abe said Japan was interested in infrastructure and human development and would assist Japanese companies entering Africa. Japan's 2017 FDI in Africa was USD 9 billion, small compared to China's USD 43 billion, but is likely to grow in the future. These developments may signal a new 'scramble for Africa'. One key to ensuring benefits for Africans is that African countries evaluate FDI and recognise they can influence the forces of trade and investment. Africa, home to over a billion people, represents a substantial potential market and source of labour and natural resources. This puts countries in a strong negotiating position.

## Conclusion

We presented the situation in African from a historical perspective and looked at geography and culture to understand the current business environment in Africa. We showed that Africa has faced challenges in its relations with the rest of the world, especially the colonisers, and these have influenced current business practices. Managers should understand that management practices are underdeveloped because of historical factors. The chapter also provided information on the situation in today's Africa, where many countries are performing well on economic measures.

## Review/Discussion

- Discuss different perceptions that people outside Africa have about Africa.
- Discuss why the business environment in Africa is still relatively underdeveloped.
- Explain why African countries are good places to do business.
- Discuss the opportunities that Africa offers to the rest of the world for investment.
- Discuss the challenges managers can expect when doing business in Africa.
- Explain the likely effect of the slave trade on current business management practices in Africa.
- Identify and discuss the impact of COVID-19 on African countries.

## Exercise

Go online and identify a successful African entrepreneur. Research this entrepreneur's business activities and prepare a one-page summary to share with the class, paying particular attention to the challenges they experienced, and how they overcame them.

## References

Chami, F. A., Françoise, G., & Sophie, M. (2002). East Africa and the Middle East relationship from the first millennium BC to about 1500 AD. *Journal des africanistes*, 72(2), 21–37.

The Economist. (2010). The true size of Africa. *The Economist*. Retrieved from www.economist.com/blogs/dailychart/2010/11/cartography.

Heywood, L. M. (2009). Slavery and its transformation in the Kingdom of Kongo 1491–1800. *The Journal of African History*, 50(1), 1–22.

Kaberuka, D. (2010). Capturing Africa's business opportunities. *McKinsey & Company*. Retrieved from www.mckinsey.com/global-themes/middle-east-and-africa/capturing-africas-business-opportunity.

Prahalad, C.K. (2006). *The Fortune at the Bottom of the Pyramid*. Upper Saddle River, N.J.: Pearson Prentice Hall.

Punnett, B. J. et al. (2019). Cultural values and management in African countries. In Sims, C. & Hall, B. (Eds.), *Cultures of the World: Past, Present and Future*. New York: Nova Publishers, 39–100.

United Nations Conference on Trade Development. (2017). Report on Africa 2017, N.Y.: United Nations.

United Nations Conference on Trade Development. (2013). *Economic development in Africa report 2013*. United Nations. Retrieved from http://unctad.org/en/PublicationsLibrary/aldcafrica2013_en.pdf.

# 2   The Management Process

## Chapter Summary

This chapter discusses the meaning of management in an organisational context. It provides a model of management (including planning, organising, staffing, directing and controlling) and explains how each stage of the model takes place. In particular, the chapter assesses management in the African context. It defines what we mean by management and provides a brief history of management thinking, and then outlines aspects of the African context that may affect the reality of the practice of management. Each component of the model is considered in more detail in terms of the African context.

---

### Learning Outcomes

After completing this chapter, you will be able to:

- explain the general concept of management,
- provide definitions of management,
- illustrate that management exists everywhere, but is influenced by context,
- describe the history of management thinking,
- identify the importance of task and people orientations for effective management,
- describe the changing nature of work in the twenty-first century,
- discuss how the environment of organisations in Africa may be different from elsewhere.
- discuss how characteristics in Africa may affect management.

Gurnek Baines (2015) found that sub-Saharans outscored European and US colleagues on intellectual flexibility, creativity, team development, drive/ambition and breadth of experience; but were

---

DOI: 10.4324/9781003017516-2

> lower on commercial/analytical/strategic thinking and growth ori-
> entation; being organised, inclusive, visionary, open, engaging,
> collaborative; emotional openness, forming close/deep bonds and build-
> ing relationships. How will these characteristics affect management?

Firstly, a definition of the term management. 'Management' is used in a variety of contexts, but it is not always clear what it means. We talk about managing the household, managing our finances, managing the economy, and so on. Our focus is managing a business/organisation. We use the term organisation predominantly, because it includes for-profit businesses, public enterprises, not-for profits, non-governmental organisations and a variety of other enterprises, large or small.

In this context, management can be defined in many ways, including 'getting things done through others', 'the process of dealing with or making the most of resources and people', 'the people leading a company or organisation', 'the responsibility for a firm or organisation'. In effect, a manager has resources, including human resources, under her or his control and she or he organises and leads these resources to achieve the organisation's objectives.

Management is the process of bringing together various types of resources and using them to realise objectives. It is a process rather than a function. A process is a set of decisions and activities or a course of action. In contrast, functions are built around specialised knowledge and understanding in a particular field, such as accounting, finance, human resources, information systems, marketing, operations and so on. Management is based on general knowledge and skills regarding coordinating and using resources to realise objectives. Management applies across functions and is necessary in accounting, finance, information systems and all activities of an organisation.

Organisations, large or small, need management. This is true in African countries as elsewhere. The general concept of management is common everywhere, but how management takes place differs depending on context. The make-up of physical and human resources, cultural beliefs, customs and values, legal and political situations and so on, all impact on how management is executed. Our objective is to explore management in the context of African countries. We use a generic model and explore how the specifics of African countries interact with the model. Where possible, we use data from African countries, and research on a particular topic (e.g. leadership). Firstly, we briefly discuss management thinking evolution in recent history.

## A Brief History of Management Thinking

The rapid development of industry in Europe and the United States in late eighteenth/early nineteenth centuries occurred with the introduction of machinery (characterised by steam power), growth of factories and mass production of manufactured goods. Earlier, most work took place in small groups or guilds, often at home with individuals working on their own and training apprentices (to take over when they were too old to continue working). Mechanisation meant that people could be employed in factory settings, and one person—a manager—was responsible for a larger group of employees. Division of labour and specialisation meant that fewer skilled workers were needed.

In the early days of industrialisation, the innovators of machines and organisations were engineers. One of the earliest formal theories of management, scientific management, was proposed by Frederick Taylor in late 1880s/early 1900s. Taylor believed that management involved the collaboration of people and machines to create value. The goal of scientific management was to optimise the outputs generated from a specific set of inputs and thus achieve efficiency. Time and motion studies determined the most efficient way to perform a task. Scientific management today is thought mechanistic and is viewed with some disfavour as it usually does not consider the human side of work; however, it is often beneficial to look at a task, and its components, to determine how to perform it most efficiently. Scientific management focused on tasks and later was termed 'theory x' management by Herzberg (1976). The underlying belief was that people worked for economic reasons and they should be paid fairly—scientific management promoted payment using a piece rate system, so those who produced more were paid more.

The Hawthorne Studies in the Muldoon 1920s, a landmark study in the United States by Mayo and Roethlisberger, refocused management thinking, incorporating socio-psychological aspects of human behaviour in organisations. The study considered the impact of the workplace on productivity. Working conditions were improved for a group of employees and resulted in increased productivity. The researchers then made conditions worse to see the impact. To everyone's surprise, productivity again improved. The conclusion was that employees responded to the attention they received. They liked management's interest in them as people. This study led to others focusing on the people side of management. Herzberg called this 'theory y' management. He argued that people do not work just for money, they enjoy working, and if managers are responsive to their needs, they will be more productive.

In the mid-twentieth century Peter Drucker (1973) developed the concept 'knowledge work' (one of his many contributions to the literature). He argued that value (the worth of a good or service) wasn't created solely by producing goods and completing tasks, but also by workers' use of information. This challenged the previous relationship between managers and subordinates and led to theories of management, emphasising motivation and engagement of employees and concern with worker satisfaction. Thinking about management changed from authority and control to more participative, coaching roles and factors such as 'emotional intelligence'. It is often said that employees are an organisation's most important resource, and managing knowledge workers depends on this attitude, because the employee takes her or his knowledge wherever she or he goes.

In organisations, both task and people aspects of management are important, and, over time, 'contingency' theories of management have developed, incorporating both task and people. Interestingly, management theories developed outside of North America and Europe (China, Japan, India— collective societies) all incorporate some form of task and people management. Most agree that managers need to pay attention to the task and getting the work done, and need concern for employees, their needs, wants and satisfaction. A contingency approach to management says that management style will vary depending on the manager, employee(s), task/work, culture and working conditions/environment. Even with knowledge workers where the person is central to task accomplishment, it remains important for managers to ensure that the work gets done. For example, a dedicated research scientist may work on her or his own and be productive, but her or his manager must ensure that she or he focuses on organisational priorities, has resources necessary to carry on research and that she or he is satisfied with working conditions, colleagues, research assistants and so on.

Today's world of work is changing, and employees may work in a network rather than the traditional hierarchical management structure. More employees work from home than in the past, and work is done virtually without meeting in person. This changes the nature of management, but management remains about getting the task done and getting it done through people. Consider some aspects of the African context and how these may influence management. Concepts of organisations were introduced through colonialism, bringing ideas developed in the west. The challenge has been to integrate African-centric ideas into management and determine how to put western concepts into practice in the African context.

## The African Context

The population of Africa is a young one. Large numbers of young people across the continent are seeking employment or starting their first jobs. Young people are likely to be more technically aware/proficient than older counterparts—they have grown up with the internet, cell phones and mobile banking—but in other ways they may be relatively unskilled, with little idea of expectations in the workplace. Managers need to pay particular attention to both task and people issues with this workforce. Young employees need training and guidance in a variety of skills. They need to understand how to perform specific tasks and may need to be closely monitored/supervised to ensure acceptable performance. Organisational rules, policies and procedures need to be explained and sanctions associated with not following these identified so new employees know what to expect. Close supervision and a task orientation can be helpful for a young employee lacking confidence or unsure. These employees also need a supportive manager, coaching/helping them overcome challenges, while encouraging them to feel a valuable part of a team, relating well to others. Young employees need to feel appreciated and will be motivated by a manager who identifies and rewards effort and productivity. This management style is one that is high on both task and people orientations.

Many African countries encourage women to join organisations and progress within them. The world is recognising that employing women throughout organisations is beneficial. Women's knowledge, skills and talents are being used and their input is creating value. Women themselves are increasingly better educated and see themselves doing valuable work and contributing to organisations. In many African countries, women have traditionally been considered wives and mothers, and their main role has been limited to the home rather than formal organisations. Women have been disproportionately represented in the informal sector and in low-paid jobs. The tendency to relegate women to domestic chores was reinforced during colonialism and continued after independence. In the changing world as equality of genders becomes the norm, men and women will both manage and be managed by people of the other gender. This can be awkward because it goes against long accepted customs, and cultural values are long-standing. In North America and Europe, particularly Scandinavia, where a similar change has been occurring for some time, the need for specific gender policies, diversity training and top management support for gender equality is recognised as critical to organisational success. Managers in a changing workplace need to clearly and explicitly acknowledge and address gender issues they face. Women and men may sometimes have different approaches and styles, and this can be a benefit. Nevertheless, the well-known 'think manager, think male' is likely to prevail for some time in African countries and some research has found that some Africans subscribe to the belief that men are better managers. These beliefs will change over time as people experience the reality of women as managers and in positions throughout organisations. Dealing with change is never easy, however.

Diversity issues are not limited to gender but include groups in society who may be marginalised because of other conditions, such as disabilities, albinism or sexual preferences. People who are considered 'different' may require special support from their organisations, and managers in modern Africa need to be aware of these diversity challenges and be able to manage them effectively.

African people are often described as exhibiting tribal/ethnic loyalties, more important than loyalty to the organisation, country and so on. These loyalties can influence aspects of management. Managers and subordinates of the same background form in-groups and those in the in-group get special favours and reciprocate through loyalty to the manager. The existence of in-groups implies out-groups who are treated less favourably. The GLOBE project on leadership identified a style which was called 'self-protective' where the manager was self-centred, status conscious and induced conflict through in-groups, and universally, survey respondents saw this style as negative. This style may be associated with ethnic/tribal loyalties and managers need to be aware of this and be proactive in avoiding the potential negative consequences.

People of certain ethnicities/tribes may be thought to have special skills and be better suited to certain jobs or better able to function as managers. This will influence the choices associated with staffing decisions and promotions. Most organisations seek to promote an equitable workplace where people believe they are treated fairly; thus, making choices based on ethnicity/tribe may be unfair. At the same time, there may be potential benefits to tribal loyalties. It may be that a person is more acceptable to members of her or his own tribe and this can be useful; for example, a salesperson going into smaller towns, villages and rural areas may be able to travel more easily if she or he is of the appropriate ethnic/tribal background. A medical person introducing vaccinations and new medicines may be more likely to meet with success if she or he is of a certain tribe. Managers can seek to use these loyalties when they are beneficial and avoid their potentially negative outcomes. These tendencies may be less strong in urban settings but remain in rural Africa and care needs to be taken to ensure that organisations take advantage of them rather than suffer from negative consequences of stereotyping.

In North America and Europe, there are laws that make it illegal to discriminate based on race, religion, gender and other factors. Discriminating in favour of/against someone of a particular ethnicity/tribe would be illegal. In Africa, favouritism, based on tribe/ethnicity, may be more common even though laws do not allow this and organisations should seek to encourage a meritocratic approach to employment.

Chapter 1 indicated that African countries were relatively high on power distance, relatively collective, moderate to somewhat high on uncertainty avoidance and masculinity and relatively low on Confucian Dynamism (long-term orientation). These values will be reflected in management styles, preferences and effectiveness. A somewhat autocratic management may be the norm with decisions made at the top and accepted by those at lower levels. In-group loyalty may be characteristic, with managers looking after their subordinates and expecting loyalty in return. Employees will like certainty and security, with clear policies, procedures and rules.

Uncertainty avoidance may also imply resistance to change. Masculinity suggests that employees will work hard to achieve tangible results and will expect rewards for these achievements and will favour men for management positions. Finally, a short-term orientation will be seen in planning, perhaps with a sense of fatalism—expressions like 'god willing' reflect this.

The next section provides a general model of the process of management. This model is a simplified way of looking at management and allows us to consider various components of management. These components can also be thought of as activities undertaken to achieve desirable outcomes for the organisation.

## A Model of Management

The following model consisting of planning, organising, staffing, directing and controlling is often used to break management into component parts. *Planning* is the beginning and leads to *Organising,* which provides the basis for *Staffing,* which results in *Directing* and the need for *Controlling.* The results of Controlling lead back to Planning, and the cycle continues. These are discussed briefly here, and in more detail in future chapters.

> *Planning:* is the beginning of the management process. To manage resources effectively, it is necessary to know what we want to achieve. This requires planning. Planning is both long-term and short-term, involving setting goals that the organisation will achieve both long term and short term. Long-term planning is referred to as strategic planning and considers the organisation and its environment to determine what it can and wants to achieve over time. It involves setting the goals to be achieved in the long term, say in five years' time (or sometimes even longer). Short-term planning refers to the more immediate, day-to-day decisions that keep the organisation running and moving in the desired direction so longer term goals will be achieved. Goals are thought of as broader and less well defined, while objectives are more quantifiable and measurable. Both long-term and short-term planning provides the building blocks of management. The manager's other activities are determined and take place because of planning.
>
> *Organising:* is the second step in the management process. This involves putting appropriate resources into place so plans can be implemented to achieve objectives. This includes analysing the work required to complete the organisation's activities, division of these activities into meaningful sets of tasks and establishing positions or sub-units responsible for carrying out the tasks. This is often depicted in an organisation chart which shows the structure of an organisation and

the relationships and relative ranks of its parts and positions/jobs. The organisation chart identifies different levels of management with reporting relationships, each set of managers reporting to a manager at the level above, down to supervisors and individuals at the lowest level. Traditional organisations are very structured with clear levels and well-defined reporting relationships. The world of work is evolving rapidly in the twenty-first century. New technologies make it possible for employees to work remotely, on their own or in virtual teams. The gig economy, as now termed, is characterised by short-term contracts or freelance work as opposed to permanent jobs. These changes in the workplace mean that traditional organisation charts are not as common as they once were. These trends are likely to be exacerbated by the Coronavirus pandemic of 2020 and onwards.

*Staffing:* involves filling positions, identified as part of the organising step, with people who carry out activities pertaining to the assigned position. Typically, a job description is prepared for each position and candidates for the position are evaluated (skills, knowledge, abilities) to determine the best person for the job; for example, for a job in a warehouse, someone may have to lift packages of a certain weight, read delivery forms, prepare invoices and shipping documents, keep track of inventory using a computer and so on. These requirements form part of a job description, which might include softer skills as well, for example, working well with others, being a good communicator and so on. Candidates for the position can then be compared and considered based on the requirements in the description.

*Directing:* can be described as behaviours and activities designed to get people to carry out the actions needed to keep the organisation running to achieve the goals set during planning. Directing encompasses communication, leadership and motivation. Effective directing ensures that goals are communicated and understood. This depends on a leadership style that appeals to followers and is key to motivating employees to want to be productive and work to achieve the organisation's goals. Directing is central to the concept of management, as it is the human side of management.

*Controlling:* involves measuring achievement against established objectives and goals. Controlling is designed to show whether the organisation is progressing as intended, so corrective action can be taken if not. Controlling leads back to planning, because controls enable managers to decide if, and how, original, and subsequent plans need to be adjusted or changed.

The model described is sequential, and iterative, progressing from one stage to another in a series of steps. Planning leads to organising; organising provides the basis for staffing; staffing results in directing; all these activities lead to performance which is monitored by controlling and compared to expectations; controlling leads back to planning. It is easy to describe the model in these terms, however, this is simplistic. The reality is that all steps interact with each other and often take place continually and simultaneously. For example, as planning takes place, it may be in the context of the organisation that exists and the staff that are available to carry out plans. Similarly, staffing decisions may partly depend on the controls that are available and the people in the organisation will influence those controls as well as the strategic direction and day-to-day activities. Management is a multi-faceted and complex process that integrates many inter-related considerations into all decisions. This is particularly true in small and family-owned organisations, where all aspects of management are essentially coincident and take place at the same time. Figure 2.1 illustrates this.

In this model, planning may be done considering the available staff and the existing leadership; the organisation chart may depend on family members' interests; controls may be a function of known abilities and accepted sanctions and so on. In a small, family-owned and operated business, it may be expected (even required) that the eldest son be in charge of financial matters (staffing); if he is known to be a gambler, certain controls will be necessary to ensure he does not use company resources for his gambling (controlling). These decisions would not be made in isolation, or sequentially, as in the simple model. They would be made interactively as in the dynamic model.

The management process is generic to all organisations. All effective organisations need to plan, to be organised, to have staff to get things done,

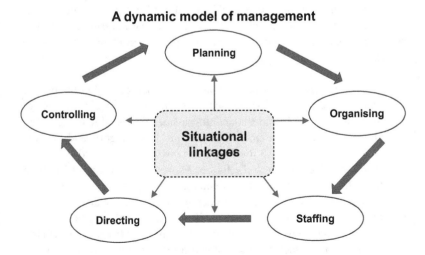

*Figure 2.1* A dynamic model of management

to direct activities through communication, leadership and motivation, and to control activities to ensure that plans are achieved, or that corrections are made. This is the case for large organisations as well as for small- or medium-sized ones. It is true for businesses whose focus is profits and for charitable and non-governmental organisations or public bodies whose purpose is not profits. It is true for family-owned businesses and co-operatives and publicly traded ones. It is even the case for the informal economy (the part of the economy that is largely unstructured and not taxed or monitored by the government). Africa's boda boda (motorcycle) transport system seems somewhat chaotic and largely unmanaged, but successful boda boda operators will plan, organise, staff, direct and control, in some sense.

Although management can be described as generic, the way management is carried out varies substantially depending on the location, people involved and their preferences, cultures and so on. Management in the United States may look substantially different from management in Africa, and management across the United States in different parts of the country may vary, and across Africa there may be divergent views of effective management. Next, we consider the African context and management.

## Management in Africa

In addition to the earlier discussion of the African context, there are several characteristics of African organisations likely to influence how management is carried out in practice. In Chapter 1, we discussed geography, culture, history and economic development, and as noted, Africa is very large and diverse, with many languages, religions, tribes/ethnicities, political systems and so on. We cannot realistically talk about Africa as a whole. Recognising this diversity, in the following discussion, we nevertheless identify some specific aspects that can influence the practice of management. Some of these:

- *Size of organisations*—many organisations, particularly in the private sector, are classified as small or medium-sized enterprises (SMEs). According to https://nextbillion.net/future-african-smes/ (accessed June 11, 2020), about 90% of African enterprises fall into this category, and in some places, it is closer to 100%. These enterprises are expected to provide much of the growth into the future. Many enterprises, particularly in the informal sector, are micro-enterprises, consisting of only a few people co-operating to get a product or service to the market.
- *Ownership of organisations*—small and micro enterprises are often family-owned and operated, or run by a group of friends, particularly in the informal sector. Larger organisations are often foreign-owned,

and recently this has included substantial Chinese investment and ownership. There are public sector organisations as well and these tend to be formal and bureaucratic.

- *Availability of infrastructure and resources*—infrastructure remains relatively limited and poor quality. Roads, bridges, ports and so on are generally not in good condition, consequently transportation is slow and cumbersome, and people cannot move around easily. Electricity and running water are limited and unavailable in most rural areas. Healthcare systems are not well-developed and constrained by inadequate numbers of trained medical personnel and modern medical equipment.
- *Demographics*—although Africa has been growing economically recently, the continent remains relatively poor, and poverty varies substantially from country to country, with some doing well and others at the bottom of the economic development ladder. Poverty has implications in terms of adequate food, housing, access to education and so on. Africa is a youthful continent and has a large available workforce, which may need training and education. Unemployment rates, particularly among youths are high.
- *Culture*—several cultural characteristics are relevant to management. We cannot outline them all but highlight two. Loyalty to the group is important in most places. This is sometimes called 'tribal loyalty' and infers that preference may be given to others of a similar background. Women remain in secondary positions in much of Africa. This is changing, with greater emphasis on gender equality, but there are few women managers, executives or directors.

These characteristics influence the management process and will be looked at in more detail in upcoming chapters.

## Conclusion

Management is likely to be found everywhere and throughout time. During human's earliest forays to hunt and gather food, someone in a position of greater power made decisions, with input from others, regarding where to hunt, when to hunt, how long to hunt and so on (planning); she or he decided what positions were needed, where older people would be, roles, and so on (organising); specific people would be assigned to roles—runners, spear throwers, fruit pickers and so on (staffing); someone ensured everyone performed their roles (directing); someone kept track of meat killed, fruit harvested, quantities used, to be sure there was enough until the next hunt/gathering (controlling). The term management, at least in English, is relatively recent, and came into common use with the industrial revolution. In this chapter, we gave a brief overview of the development of thinking about management from the industrial revolution to the present. This discussion is essentially from a 'western' perspective, because most management research and literature are from this perspective. The industrial revolution meant that predominantly agrarian, rural societies in Europe and America became industrial and urban, and, in ways, this is true of current-day Africa, so there are lessons for African management that can be gleaned from the development of management thinking in the West. In this chapter, we have highlighted aspects of the African context that are likely to influence the reality of management in Africa.

## Exercise

### *Plus One*

*Contributed by Thomas Senaji, Ali Taleb and Don Wood*

Africa is very diverse, and some diversities are well documented, notably ethnic diversity; however, there are others not documented, which manifest themselves in interactions within the African context. To capture additional salient diversities, we developed the metaphor 'Plus One'.

'Plus One' means that there is something extra that should anticipate and build a capability to deal with unexpected eventualities. Besides knowing how many tribes/ethnic groups there are in African countries, there are unique aspects within the cultures of these communities, such as the high propensity to trust in-groups (members of own ethnic group) more than outgroups. When you are a member of the in-group, you are treated preferentially. For example, the award of business contracts and sharing of critical business information are more likely among in-group members compared to those in the out-group. The criterion for being in the in-group is predominantly ethnicity and to a less extent religion.

In recognition of diversity Kenya promulgated the Constitution of Kenya, 2010, to address diversity, mainly in terms of gender, regional balance and ethnicity, in public employment. Notwithstanding, there are emerging issues that management and business need to consider to succeed in Kenya. For instance, formal rules, regulations and laws exist but informal institutions, social norms, religion, beliefs and in some cases stereotypes, are important in cross-border trade and trust is more relevant for conducting business than formal contracts. This is what is meant by 'Plus One'. We can describe Kenya as 43+1 meaning that there are 43 tribes/ethnic communities but there is something else we do not know specifically, and which we need to incorporate into doing business in Kenya. For example, how to recruit and hire new employees in a manner that addresses the ethnicities of potential candidates.

Managers and business in the region should consider the informal institutions and societal dynamics in hiring, marketing, leadership approaches and decision-making by going beyond the known, and anticipating and incorporating emerging 'plus one' issues.

### *Assignments*

- Identify a 'plus one' situation that you are familiar with, in a business setting, and explain how it should be addressed, to succeed in the African business environment.
- How can we deal with the tension between in-group and out-group considerations in a typical management situation?
- What are the implications for working within an in-group/out-group? Does it lead to tensions? How do you overcome these?

## Review/Discussion

- Discuss the concept and model of management and its five components.
- Identify two aspects of the African context that are important to effective management and discuss how they relate to management.
- Discuss the following 'the western concept of management does not apply in the African context'.
- 'Tribalism' is often considered a typical characteristic of African countries. Define 'tribalism' and discuss its negative consequences for organisations.
- 'Gender inequality is still a problem in management in Africa'. Discuss this statement.

## References

Baines, G. (2015). Leadership across cultures. *Harvard Business Review*, May 30–31.

Drucker, P. F. (1973). *Management: Tasks, Responsibilities, Practices*. New York: Harper & Row.

Herzberg, F. (1976). *The Managerial Choice: To Be Efficient and to Be Human*. Homewood, IL: Dow Jones-Irwin.

Muldoon, J. (2012). The Hawthorne legacy: A reassessment of the impact of the Hawthorne studies on management scholarship, 1930–1958. *Journal of Management History*, 18(1), 105–119.

# 3 Planning

## Chapter Summary

Do you have a plan? What is the plan? These are common questions people ask when they want to know something about the future. That future might be a few hours away, a day, a week, months or even years. In this chapter, we present the subject of planning in the context of existing business organisations, such as companies, partnerships and sole proprietorships. The planning processes that we describe also apply to many kinds of organisations, including public corporations, nongovernmental organisations, trusts, foundations, as well as small, family-owned ones. Large organisations, such SABMiller, the South African beer-producing company, or Dangote Group, the Nigerian company that produces and supplies a range of products, need planning, and small companies such as Plasco Tanzania, which manufactures and sells water pipes need planning.

---

### Learning Outcomes

After completing this chapter, you will be able to:

- explain the meaning of planning,
- discuss the evolution of planning,
- compare and contrast different types of plans,
- describe the importance of planning in business organisations,
- define key terminologies used in planning,
- define and explain the concept of SMART objectives.

One manager told one of the authors that 'I have been called by the directors who are also the owners of the company to discuss with them issues about the company, even though I am not the CEO. But all this depends on trust'.

---

DOI: 10.4324/9781003017516-3

## The Role and Importance of Planning

The word 'plan' entered the English world in the seventeenth century from Latin, *planus* meaning 'flat'. This suggests that previously there was no planning in the business context. Yet this process is so important in business. When the word was used in English, it meant a drawing or sketch projecting an object on a flat surface and meant the same as *'blueprint'*.

Planning is the process or activity of preparing a plan and has various elements. It is a mental activity involving thinking. It specifies things to be achieved, what to do to achieve them, where and who are responsible for doing what. A plan can be defined as a document containing goals and objectives to be achieved to realise the mandate of an organisation. It specifies the resources, human and financial, required to implement objectives and goals. Planning involves selection of alternatives for every activity so in the end the goals and objectives are achieved. Planning is concerned with the future and is essentially the image of the future. The extent of futurity depends on organisational level—operational managers deal with a closer, more immediate future (days, weeks, months) and executives deal with a more distant future (three, five or more years). Henry Fayol, an early management scholar used *'prevoyance'* meaning to *'foresee'*, implying future assessment and provisions for it. Planning originated from the military where the term was commonly used before it became common in business in the twentieth century.

In demonstrating the importance of planning, Henry Fayol (Cleland, 1962) said:

> The Maxim, 'Managing means looking ahead' gives some idea of the importance attached to planning in the business world and it is true that if foresight is not the whole of management, at least it is an essential part of it. . . . The most effective instrument of planning is the plan of action . . . is at one and the same time, the result of envisaged, the line of action to be followed, the stages to go through, and the methods to use.

Planning is important because it ensures organisations have goals and objectives to achieve; planning helps organisations chart direction, based on goals. Goals represent the outcomes to be achieved to attain the reasons for the organisation's existence. Each organisation is established for a reason, constituting its mandate, and to achieve this, managers set goals to accomplish this mandate. In a profit-making organisation, making profits for shareholders are usually assumed to be the goals. For non-profit organisations goals will be provision of certain services—the mission of World Vision, an international NGO with country offices in about 100 countries, is to provide humanitarian services (helping to feed children by supporting families to improve their economic well-being) and goals will be based on this mission.

Planning is important for identifying activities/tasks to be performed and assigning responsibilities for these. This facilitates effective coordination. Activities and tasks are related, but different. An activity is something that must be done to achieve a goal and may include several tasks. Tasks are more specific, leading to accomplishment of an activity. A company with the mission of making profits to pay dividends to shareholders needs to sell/provide enough goods/services to customers. This does not occur automatically, it requires activities including advertising, making calls to/visiting customers, delivering goods, among others. To accomplish these, certain tasks must be undertaken, including, hiring an adverting company, engaging a TV station to run advertisements, transporting goods, providing services, sending invoices and so on.

Defining activities and tasks is not enough; they must be assigned to specific individuals. If not, no-one will feel responsible for performing them and they will not get done. Time frames for completing tasks/activities need to be established. This involves deciding how much time is needed to complete a certain task or activity. The planning process ensures relevant tasks/activities to reach goals are identified and assigned to appropriate individuals. The planning process can also identify ways to improve the way a business is organised.

Planning allows management to identify resources/inputs required to implement defined activities, including human and non-human (equipment, funds, etc.) resources. During planning, sources of these resources are identified. The planning process shows whether the organisation has resources to reach its goals. If the goal is to expand production, planning will reveal if additional machinery is needed and so on. Efficient allocation of resources can be achieved through planning, preventing arbitrary use of resources and avoiding duplication of effort. This facilitates learning in terms of inputs required for production/provision of goods/services.

Planning facilitates the exercise of control. Control ensures the organisation stays on course to achieve its goals, by comparing actual results with planned results and taking corrective action, if substantially different. If a profit-making organisation planned to achieve a profit USD1 billion, but made a profit of USD0.9 billion, the company failed to meet its goal. The actual performance of the organisation was below that expected, and managers need to identify why.

Managers and staff draw motivation from the plans to be implemented; a plan provides goals that they will strive to achieve. Without a plan with clearly defined goals, managers and staff have no incentive to work hard; they do not know what level of performance is required. Research shows that goals, especially clear ones, motivate people to exert efforts to reach those goals.

Planning promotes a culture of learning because the process involves collecting, processing and analysing data from inside and outside the organisation to provide information. New knowledge about the organisation's progress is generated, with benefits, including encouraging innovation and sustaining organisational competitiveness. The process contributes to improved performance by generating relevant information for better environmental understanding and reducing uncertainty.

## The Planning Process

Planning and the resulting output can be categorised on a time dimension and organisational hierarchy level. Three terms that are commonly used for planning are strategic, tactical and operational planning. Organisations prepare and implement over-arching strategic plans (long-range/term). Those incorporate tactical plans and operational plans (short-range/term). Strategic planning emphasises wide-ranging implications of the outcomes of the process. Tactical planning and operational planning are constituent elements of the planning process. In practice, the categorisation of the planning process communicates the timeframe and level in the organisation where the planning takes place, whether at the apex, middle or operational level.

Figure 3.1 shows the levels at which planning takes place to produce different outputs. Strategic planning is usually the prerogative of senior management, consisting of the chief executive officer (CEO) and other members of management such as heads of division, departments and so on, depending on how senior management is defined. In some cases, especially in small business in Africa, members of the board of directors participate in strategic planning processes.

*Figure 3.1* Management triangle showing levels at which different types of plans are prepared.

## Strategic versus Long-Term/Range Planning

The output of strategic planning (also referred to as long-range/term planning) is a strategic plan or a long-range/term plan. One source may use the term 'strategic' in a discussion while another uses long-term or long-range, yet the context of discussions may be similar. This can be confusing, and we want to be clear with these terms. While used interchangeably, they have different connotations. Long-range planning was used earlier, followed by strategic planning; in this sense, strategic planning, is an improved version of long-range planning.

Long-term/range planning emerged in business in the twentieth century, but the term had been used in other fields especially defence/military. Long-range planning and plans emerged from the public sector in the 1950s–1960s when countries began to make economic development plans covering four or five years. In business, they were considered an extension of regular one-year financial planning, including budgets and operating plans. Plans were prepared without attention to changes in the environment, such as the social, economic and political environments.

Long-range planning assumes that the present knowledge will apply to future conditions and extrapolates the present into the future, as if future conditions will remain constant. Long-range planning is based on predicting the future from historical evolution. If a firm produces 400 tons per year of flour, and management wants to know what production will be over three years, they simply multiply 4,000 by 3. Other variables related to production will be extended at current levels. Long-range planning tends to be bottom-up, a consolidation of plans from individual units, and numbers driven. Long-range is two years or longer, with four being common, while mid-range would be one year.

Due to shortcomings of this approach, improvements were introduced into the planning process, to consider potential changes in the future, such as product and market development, diversification, business growth and environmental shifts. The new approach was considered more strategic, hence strategic planning, which became more common and important in the mid-1960s. Its main feature was environmental analysis, to arrive at a strategic diagnosis of the company. Strategic planning assumes that an organisation needs to respond quickly to a dynamic, changing environment, which may require alterations and shifts. The focus is on making decisions that ensure the organisation's ability to respond successfully to changes in the environment.

Strategic planning is a systematic procedure for envisioning a desired future and translating this vision into broadly characterised goals and objectives, with a sequence of steps to accomplish them. It is idea driven, more qualitative and seeks to provide a clear organisational vision and focus. Strategic planning deliberately attempts to concentrate resources in those areas that may produce substantial improvements in future capacity and performance. A strategic plan is a road map to lead an organisation from where it is now to where it would like to be in the future. The time frame for strategic plans varies between two and ten years, with five years being the most common.

## Tactical Planning

Tactical planning takes place at the middle management level (see Figure 3.1). It translates the vision and goals of the organisation into objectives and actions. Once senior management and members of the board of directors (where they participate) have laid out the vision and defined broad goals, middle managers determine how their respective departments will participate in achieving the goals and the vision. On the basis of the goals, these managers develop actions they will implement, to contribute towards achieving the strategic goals. The output of tactical planning is an action plan, with objectives, meeting the SMART test and actions to attain the objectives. SMART is specific, measurable, attainable, relevant and time-bound. Specificity means objectives are sufficiently precise and unambiguous; measurable that they are quantified; attainable that they are realistic; relevant that they lead to attainment of the goals of the organisation; time-bound that there is a timeframe for realisation.

## Operational Planning

Operational plans are usually developed by middle-level managers in consultation with lower level managers and staff, based on tactical plans. They are prepared by departments to operationalise the tactical plan, make it practically implementable. They outline what individual units, for example departments or sections will focus on in the immediate future. The strategic plan provides the vision for the future and direction through goals, the tactical plan provides milestones in terms of objectives and the operational plan lays out what will be done on a daily to weekly basis to reach the anticipated future, that is, realisation of objectives and goals. Operational plans are important; without them, implementation is haphazard and may not lead to attainment of goals in the strategic plan. Operational plans lead to implementation by translating strategic and tactual plans into specific activities for functional areas. Firms, including small ones, engage in operational planning and it is important for enterprises of all sizes, although small firms may be less enthusiastic about formal planning. Even through small firms have limited resources they still need to prepare operational plans and even when there is no strategic plan, operational planning is needed to manage resources effectively.

An operational plan is a practical plan of activities and concrete enough so managers and employees at each level understand their specific responsibilities. It describes tactics to be employed as the preferred method for achieving objectives or targets. Based on the strategic and the tactical plans, the operational plan provides answers to the following:

- Which departments and personnel are responsible for realisation of which goals?
- What activities and tasks are each department and employee responsible for?
- Where will daily operations take place?
- What are the estimates, costs or budget that must be allocated to each department to complete defined tasks?
- What are the deadlines for the completion of each task?

Plan should include:

- A description of activities and a statement as to which major objective of the strategic plan it falls under.
- The timing and sequencing of activities.
- The number of activities.
- The person(s) responsible for each activity.
- The resources required, including financial resources, and the origin of those resources.
- A method of measuring progress (monitoring).

## Strategic Planning Steps

Here, we adapt the process described by Bryson (1998) and other relevant literature. The steps are initiating and agreeing on a process in the context of organisational mandates; assessing the external and internal environments; clarifying organisational mission, vision and values; defining goals and objectives; specifying activities and tasks; establishing inputs and respective costs. Figure 3.2 shows the steps.

### *Initiating and Agreeing on Process*

This covers agreement on the purpose; preferred steps; the form and timing of reports; the role, functions and membership of a coordinating team (such as a committee); the role, functions and membership of the strategic planning team; commitment of necessary resources to proceed. Discussions of the mandates of the organisation should occur because the planning process cannot be implemented outside the mandates, defined by establishing instruments.

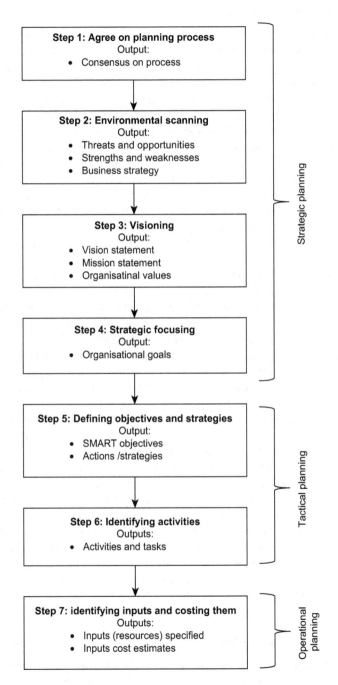

*Figure 3.2* Strategic planning steps

### Environmental Scanning

This involves assessing the operating internal and external environments. Scanning the external environment identifies issues originating outside the organisation that may affect the business. This involves gathering and analysing information to help management understand and identify the issues, challenges and trends that will shape and affect the business, including information about target customers, competitors and suppliers, among others. The process includes reviewing literature, identifying and analysing organisations working on similar issues or in the same geographic region, interviewing experts in the field and related fields. The PEST model is commonly employed in environmental scanning. PEST stands for political, economic, social and technological factors that affect your organisation's mission and approach. Recently, some authors talk of the PESTLE model, adding legal and environmental factors.

Scanning the internal environment means looking inward to understand issues that may affect strategy. The most common internal analysis method is the SWOT. SWOT stands for strengths, weaknesses, opportunities and threats. A SWOT analysis summarises perceptions of an internal constituency (leadership and staff) regarding the strengths and weaknesses of the firm, the external opportunities for potential pursuit and the external threats to consider. This analysis considers the capacity to deliver the intended products/services, core competencies (what the entity is fundamentally good at doing), business processes (how work gets done), staffing (roles, skills, knowledge), assets (e.g. buildings, equipment) and financial resources (e.g. budget).

PESTLE and SWOT are used to assess the external and internal environments respectively; Porter's five forces model is often used to determine the intensity of competition in an industry. According to Porter (1979), the five forces that affect an industry are competition in the industry, the threat of new entrants, the bargaining power of buyers, the threat from substitutes and the bargaining power of suppliers. Organisations may also use the value chain analysis (Porter, 1985) to understand internal processes of generating value so that it can formulate a strategy that will enable it to compete effectively. To be effective, business firms usually have to choose between cost leadership strategies and differentiation strategies. Readers are advised to review these types of strategies and their implications for business as detailed in business strategy formulation textbooks.

### Vision, Mission and Values

Once the external and internal inputs are analysed, management is ready to set the overall vision, mission and values of the organisation:

*Vision:* Vision statements play the role of a strategic 'north star', providing focus and long-term alignment. The vision is a set of words that announce what the company or organisation hopes to be. The vision defines the organisation's highest aspirations, explains why it is in a particular business, indicates the desired characteristics of the business in the future and identifies the goals and objectives most crucial to achieving the shared vision of the future. A vision statement expresses in plain and simple language what the organisation intends to accomplish. For example:

- Dangote Group's: To be a global leader in cement production, respected for the quality of our products and services and for the way we conduct our business.
- Simba Cement's: To be Eastern Africa's preferred cement manufacturer and distributor.

*Mission:* Mission statements identify the purpose of the business, who the customers are, how the organisation operates. Once a stakeholder analysis is completed, the organisation can develop a mission statement that takes key stakeholder interests into account. For example:

- Dangote Cement's: To deliver strong returns to shareholders by selling high-quality products at affordable prices, backed by excellent customer service.
- Tanga Cement's: To develop, produce and distribute consistently high-quality cement and related products and services in a sustainable manner to satisfy our customers' expectations.

*Values:* Values are a set of beliefs and principles that exist behind the scenes to guide the activities and the organisation's operations. Every organisation has values forming the foundation for its activities, which act as 'core' beliefs. Values underpin the culture of the organisation and play a role in shaping business strategies. Many companies and other organisations post their values on their websites and include them in annual reports. For example, the values of Dangote Groups are: respect, teamwork, empowerment, inclusion, integrity, learning and meritocracy (Dangote Annual Report, 2018). Simba Cement's values are people (acting with integrity and respect); planet (responsible approach to the community) and environment and performance (to be the best in everything we do).

## Defining Goals for the Organisation

Goals are statements that describe where the organisation wants to be in the future, indicating long-term commitments and priorities. Goals do not explain how to get to that future and goals are often large in scope or size and possibly somewhat intangible. An example of a goal for a university might be 'to increase student enrolment'. A mobile phone company such as Airtel may have a goal 'to increase users of Airtel money'. Although these are good goals, there are no specific timeframes or actions that guide employees on how to achieve them. They would be better goals if they were more specific. For example, to increase student enrolment by 10% a year for the next five years (for a university) and to increase use of Airtel money from 1 million to 1.5 million over the next three years (in the case of Airtel).

Goals can be divided into three types—service goals, resource management goals and administrative/directional goals. Service goals specify the types and levels of service to be provided and resource goals state the resource levels required to achieve the service goals. Administrative goals deal with developments in the organisation and future planning activities; for example, 'To make library collections more relevant to the needs of users'. In defining goals, some of the questions that must be addressed include:

- What is the core competency of the organisation?
- Where do we want our business to be one year from now, three to five years from now?
- What are our competitors' strengths and weaknesses and how can they be adapted or exploited?
- What do our existing and potential customers want?
- Are any current or developing niches in our target market not being exploited?
- What opportunities and threats should we consider?
- What are our strengths and weaknesses and how can we use our strengths and overcome our weaknesses?
- Do we have the resources to get to our goals?

Ideas, suggestions and information, including market intelligence, from lower levels of the organisational hierarchy are included in the planning process through the heads of departments. Heads of departments obtain input from others within the department and share them at strategic planning meetings. These inputs, with additional input from senior management and directors (who may also be owners), are further debated and refined at planning meetings to arrive at the vision, mission, values and goals. The next steps, defining objectives, activities and tasks constitute tactical planning.

### *Defining Objectives*

Objectives are the specific actions and measurable steps to take to reach stated goals. Objectives give a clear understanding of the specific activities to be completed to reach goals. Objectives must be relevant to the goals to which they relate and be SMART. This helps to ensure that objectives can be monitored to ensure that they are being achieved. An example of a goal and related objectives:

- Goal: To make library collections more relevant to the needs of users.

  - Objective: To increase to 15% the proportion of the total budget spent on materials.
  - To spend 20% of the annual materials budget for subscriptions.

The objectives will also serve as performance measures. For example, using the first objective stated previously, information will be collected at the end of a given period to establish the proportion of the budget used on materials and compare it with the original objective of 15%.

### *Defining Activities and Tasks*

Activities ensure the delivery of a strategy and include specific tasks that have start dates, end dates, owners and deliverables. Activities produce a clear, measurable impact on the objectives to which they are aligned. Performance measures indicate success of the initiative(s) by displaying impact and achievement for the objective. Once goals, objectives, activities and tasks have been defined, an organisation has a strategy in place. The next step is operational planning where detailed inputs and their respective costs are established.

### *Inputs and Respective Costs*

After the aforementioned stapes are complete, they are combined into a written document. In this step, each unit or department takes the strategic plan and develops its own plan for implementation. During the process of defining input and the associated costs, care must be taken to consider the following issues:

- How departmental staff will be optimally allocated to execute plans effectively and efficiently.
- How financial resources will be acquired and allocated to maximise returns and value for money.

Following agreement within the department, an operation plan is prepared. An example of an extract of an operational plan is given in Figure 3.3.

| Goal: Meet customer demand | | | | | | | | | | | | | | | |
|---|---|---|---|---|---|---|---|---|---|---|---|---|---|---|---|
| **Objective: Increase production by 15% over the next three years** | | | | | | | | | | | | | | | |
| Success factors/ KPI | Strategies | Activities or programs | Time frame | | | | | | | | | | | Responsible persons | Budget | |
| | | | Q1 | | | Q2 | | | Q3 | | | Q4 | | | Amount | Source |
| | | | J | F | M | A | M | J | J | A | S | O | N | D | | |
| Increased number of units produced by 5% annually | Increase production | ◆ Buy new machine<br><br>◆ Increase materials stocked<br><br>◆ Expand warehouse | | | | | | | | | | | | | | |
| | | | | | | | | | | | | | | | | |
| | | | | | | | | | | | | | | | | |

*Figure 3.3* Operational plan

## African Context

Strategic planning is a top management activity, focusing on the long term and setting out the organisation's vision, mission and values, giving it an overall purpose. In larger organisations, particularly in the west, strategy is seen as a somewhat formal and structured endeavour. This would also be true in large business organisations in Africa such as subsidiaries of multi-nationals based in Europe of North America. The informal sector is important in the African context, and many business organisations are small and family-owned. In this situation, formal, structured strategic planning may be rare or non-existent. This does not mean that organisations will be successful if they have no plans. Planning is a critical component of good management; however, it may be approached differently in this context. Anecdotal evidence and informal discussions with managers of African businesses show that in small businesses, board members who are also usually owners tend to be very involved in the strategic planning process. During the planning, they join senior management in defining the mission, vision and goals of the organisation. These shareholders/directors are involved in the first four steps of the process presented earlier; however, they are often not involved in tactical and operational planning. Once the planning process is complete, they then take part in approving the plans and the budgets when management presents them to the board.

Another aspect of planning in African businesses, especially small ones, is that the process is informal and there are often no written guidelines regarding the process. This may be confusing for managers who are experienced in planning in large companies that follow western ways of management, where processes are highly formalised, for example there is a planning calendar, with detailed written steps for the process. Instead, the planning process may be triggered by a major event; for example, the reality that a new financial year is about to start and forms from tax authorities have to be completed, showing estimated profits for the next financial year. Management may start planning so they can complete forms and return them to tax authorities. Revisions of plans may also be triggered by major environmental event, for example, many organisations have reviewed their strategic plans due to the breakout of the COVID-19 pandemic.

The informality of the planning process and other managerial functions also means that shareholders/owners may reach out directly to the lower level managers to ask for information and ideas. This is dependent on a degree of trust.

## Conclusion

In this chapter, we presented the concept of planning including three types of plans: strategic, tactical and operational. Strategic planning and operational planning are applied in the context of existing businesses (note that business plan development applies to new businesses or the expansion of a business and precedes other management activities). Planning started as long-range planning and evolved into strategic planning. We discussed a model of planning activities and explained the steps in the planning process. We also discussed strategic planning in the African context as characterised by informality, and with substantial involvement of owners, with trust underpinning many aspects of management, including planning.

## Review/Discussion

1.  Discuss the meaning and benefits of planning.
2.  Discuss how strategic planning is different from operational planning.
3.  'Only large companies need to plan'. Discuss this assertation.
4.  Identify and discuss some unique conditions or factors that influence planning in businesses in the African context.

## Exercise

TBL is the largest Tanzanian beer producer and distributer. The company engages in strategic planning periodically. The TBL's annual report for 2018 contains a list of strategic objectives that are listed subsequently. These are:

a.   To partner with the government and other stakeholders to spearhead a positive environment for socio-economic growth.

b.   To enhance our ability to influence consumer and retailer buying decisions by continually improving customer service levels, providing consumers with greater access to our full brand portfolio and providing consumers with optimal value for money products.

c.   To promote local sourcing of raw materials; this not only improves our efficiencies but also supports the development of the communities across the region.

d.   To grow and develop our greatest strength, our people and as such reward them accordingly.

e.   To recruit, retain, develop and reward the best talents accordingly.

f.   To manage our costs tightly, to free up resources that will support sustainable and profitable top line growth.

Based on discussions in this chapter, comment on the strategic objectives of the TBL.

## References

Bryson, J. M. (1998). A strategic planning process for public and non-profit organizations. *Long Range Planning*, 21(1), 73–81.

Cleland, D. I. (1962). *The origin and development of a philosophy of long-range planning in American business*. A PhD dissertation, Ohio State University, USA.

Porter, M. E. (1979). How competitive forces shape strategy. *Harvard Business Review*, March/April.

Porter, M. E. (1985). *Competitive Advantage*. New York: Free Press.

# 4   Organising

## Chapter Summary

Organising follows from planning and involves designing and maintaining a system that coordinates activities, individually and cooperatively, to achieve organisational goals. Management defines tasks and assigns them to individuals/groups. Management determines how people relate to one another, clarifying authority/reporting relationships so activities are implemented smoothly. Management establishes roles and responsibilities for completion of tasks required to meet goals. Organising leads to a structure, which provides guidance on the division of work into activities, linkages between different functions, hierarchy, authority relationships and coordination. This chapter discusses concepts, theories, principles and types/forms of organisational structures.

---

### Learning Outcomes

After completing this chapter, you will be able to:

- Define an organisational structure.
- Describe the process of organising.
- Discuss the theories and principles involved in organising.
- Explain the importance of organising.
- Discuss different forms of organisational structure.
- Apply the generic theories of organisations in the African context.

I worked for a small company in Africa, owned by and making parts for a company in the United States. In Africa, there was a manager responsible for the entire operation, to whom everyone reported. There was a man with some technical expertise who oversaw the machinery, kept track of inventory, arranged shipments and so on, someone trained in quality control, and a driver. There were about 100 workers who produced the parts. In the United States, as

---

DOI: 10.4324/9781003017516-4

I understood it, it was a very small organisation. The owner was the CEO and 'salesforce', his wife did the bookkeeping and accounts, there was a technical person who worked out the production details, a person who coordinated production among subsidiaries (there were several like ours) and an administrative assistant. We were supposed to be a 'stand-alone' operation responsible for costs and revenues, but we weren't because all sales came through the United States. The owner would skype almost every day and want to know details of 'what we were doing'—which parts we were producing, who was working, what we had in inventory and so on. Whoever happened to be in the office when the skype call came had to spend an hour talking to him. It drove us all crazy. We just wanted to get on with the work.

## Theories of Organisation

Three main theories of organisation are:

- Classical theories include scientific management (Taylor, 1947), bureaucratic management (Weber, 1947) and administrative theory (Fayol, 1949). These deal with formal organisations and ways to increase effectiveness and efficiency.
- Neoclassical theories developed in the mid-twentieth century include administrative behaviour and organisations as social networks. These deal, respectively, with decision-making in formal organisations and social aspects including goals, survival, organisational boundaries and contradictions.
- Modern theories post-1950 include a systems approach, a socio-technical approach and a contingency approach. These consider organisations as complex entities, which are dynamic and adapt to their environment, and the interplay among various aspects of the organisation.

There are several different approaches for organising. Next, we discuss principles for organising.

## Principles for Organising

The previous theories suggest broad principles for designing a structure. These are specialisation, coordination, decentralisation/centralisation and line/staff relationships. These are discussed next considering how these principles apply in the African context, in line with the general African view of organisational relationships.

## *Specialisation*

According to the classical approach, work can be performed best if divided into components and individuals specialise on specific ones; applying specialised knowledge and encouraging its development. The result is improvement in quality and quantity of work and efficiency and effectiveness. We know that if we focus on a particular task, kicking a goal and practice, we get better at it. This principle is applied in organisations through specialisation.

African communities in the past, and currently, have had diverse skills applied in different settings, including tool making, livestock keeping, farming and so on, and individuals/groups focused on one task, so skills improved through performing the same task repeatedly. During the colonial era, specialisation, especially in formal settings, was reinforced through bureaucratic procedures where employees had clearly defined, limited tasks. While specialisation works in Africa, today's organisations may require employees who are more multi-faceted than in the past.

## *Coordination*

Coordination integrates objectives and activities of specialised departments to realise the organisation's goals. It ensures synchronised activities so that implementation of one set of activities does not conflict with others. This involves placing together decisions pertaining to units/groups, along with patterns of relationships and information/communication networks. One mechanism for coordination is hierarchy—identifying relative levels within the organisation (above, at the same level, below); that is, a superior above a subordinate, who is at the same level as co-workers. Hierarchy facilitates vertical coordination of units or departments and their activities. For a hierarchy to be useful the following are important:

a.  Unity of command: Each person is responsible to one superior and receives orders from that person only, thus confusion between managers is avoided. Fayol (1949) considered this the most important principle for efficiency and increased productivity.
b.  Scalarity: Decision-making authority and the chain of command flows in a straight line from the highest level to the lowest. This is related to unity of command; however, at times horizontal communication involving people at the same level in the hierarchy takes place, and prior information to superiors is required to avoid confusion.
c.  Responsibility and authority: Responsibility is accompanied by authority to motivate and enable successful performance of tasks. Those employees who are responsible for performance of tasks should have

the appropriate level of influence on the decision-making processes that affect their performance.

d.  Span of control: The number of specialised activities or individuals that can be supervised by one person. The span of control is important for coordinating different types of activities effectively. There is no optimal number of subordinates to be supervised by one manager/ supervisor, because different factors are involved. Some important factors affecting span of control are:

   i.  Similarity of functions—the greater the similarity, the broader the span of control.
   ii.  Proximity of functions to each other and to the supervisor—the physically closer the subordinates are to the supervisor, the broader the span of control.
   iii.  Complexity of functions—the less complex the functions the broader the span of control.
   iv.  Direction and control needed—the less need for direction and control, the broader the span of control.
   v.  Coordination within a unit and between units—the lower the need for coordination, the broader the span of control.
   vi.  Extent of planning—the lower the detailed planning required, the broader the span of control.
   vii.  Organisational decision-making help—more help enables broader span of control.

e.  Stability and adaptability: There is a need to balance stability against adaptability. Organisational structures should be adaptable to environmental changes but remain steady during unfavourable conditions. Due to changing environments, organisations must be ready to adapt to new situations, including changing structures. At the same time, the existing structure provides a known framework for implementing change.

The principle of coordination presents some challenges in the African context. In many African societies, age is prioritised over knowledge and skills. Younger people are required to respect older people and not to give them orders/instruction. Wisdom and knowledge are believed to develop as one ages and older people are consulted on important issues. When younger people are in higher positions in the hierarchy, due to qualifications (e.g. a university degree), it may be difficult to function effectively and older people in lower positions may find it hard to take orders from younger superiors. Application of this principle may create tension and demotivation in the workplace. This may be further complicated by gender considerations.

This means, in designing organisational structure, care must be taken to deal with these cultural situations.

## *Centralisation/Decentralisation*

Decentralisation means decision-making takes place at lower levels while centralisation means decision-making is at higher levels of the organisation. The degree of centralisation/decentralisation depends on the number of levels in the hierarchy, specialisation, degree of coordination and span of control. Centralisation/decentralisation also depends on geographical concentration/dispersion of operations and functions and the extent of concentration or delegation of decision-making powers. For example, the management of Tanzania Cigarette, a subsidiary of Japan Tobacco International (headquartered in Switzerland), makes decisions on employment, based on local laws in Tanzania—decentralisation by geographical dispersion. Schools/colleges at the University of Dar es Salaam make decisions on using 70% of funds from various sources, based on the local situation—decentralisation by extent of concentration of power. Depending on the breadth of decentralised decisions, units will often be considered as cost centres, profit centres, or investment centres for accountability purposes—units are accountable for costs, profits or returns on investments.

Decentralisation has advantages and disadvantages. Positively, decentralisation allows faster, less costly decision-making and decisions reflect local needs and are more relevant/responsive. Negatively, decentralisation can lead to goal incongruence between higher and lower levels of the organisation, and promote parochial decision-making, focusing on the local level rather than organisation-wide concerns.

In Africa where decision-making traditionally is done by elders/people with authority, and these decisions are not questioned, decision-making is likely to be centralised. The African workforce is young and enters the workplace with greater technical knowhow and exposure to world views, and this may suggest that greater decentralisation will be welcomed or even expected by these employees. The world of work generally is changing and becoming more decentralised. The COVID-19 pandemic 2019 and on encouraged those who could, to work at home, and this meant decentralising. In the future, African organisations may be more decentralised than in the past.

## *Line and Staff Relationships*

Line authority is the scalar chain, or the superior-subordinate linkages that extend throughout the hierarchy. Line employees are responsible for achieving the basic organisational objectives and goals, while staff employees play a supporting role, providing services needed to accomplish line tasks. For example, accounting departments provide information rather than contributing directly to producing goods/services that are sold, thus it is a staff function. The line/staff relationship is crucial in organisational structure, design and efficiency, because together they enable the organisation to achieve its goals. Staff employees may be specialised, general or organisational. Specialised staff conduct technical work, such as market research and forecasting; general staff are assistants to whom managers assign projects; organisational staff provide services to the whole organisation, such as human resources, accounting and public relations.

## Types of Structures

The process described results in an organisational structure. This refers to the formal configuration between individuals and groups, regarding the allocation of tasks, responsibilities and authority within the organisation to form units/departments. These may be characterised by marketing, sales, advertising, manufacturing, finance or other activities. Within departments, distinctions are made regarding the jobs people perform. Departments are then linked to form the organisational structure.

The structure is the framework of reporting relationships, reflecting the division of work into activities and tasks. These relationships are shown on a diagram called an organisation chart. The chart depicts formal reporting relationships; in practice, informal ones exist alongside, but are not shown on the chart, as it is virtually impossible to capture these.

There are different types of structure, reflecting management's thinking and it reveals how senior management views the nature and key activities of the business; they may emphasise functions, geography, product, customers or a mixture. Organisational structure includes the following: simple, functional, product, customer, geographic, divisional, matrix, amorphous and hybrid. We briefly illustrate these.

### *Simple Structure*

Simple structures use direct supervision and employs vertical and horizontal centralisation. The organisation consists of the top manager and a few workers. Simple structures do not have a technostructure, support staff is limited and workers often perform overlapping tasks. This is common among small businesses including restaurants, shops and simple manufacturing. Most of the informal businesses dominating African countries have a simple structure. Other examples are small owner-managed companies, new government departments and small privately-owned schools. This usually changes as the organisation grows and often a functional structure is adopted. The simplicity means the more formal principles of management may not necessarily apply to organisations with a simple structure.

### *Functional Structure*

Functional structures group jobs and activities involving common functions. Work is divided according to the nature of activities performed, requiring specialised skills, including, marketing, finance, production, administration, research and development and so on. The assumption is that strategic organisational capabilities lie in functional skills and emphasis on specialisation. Figure 4.1 is an example of a functional structure.

### Advantages of the functional structure

*   Specialisation and mastery of activities involved in the functions.
*   Employees joining the organisation at lower levels develop expertise and become highly qualified in their specialisation.
*   People inside and outside the organisation know whom to call for particular needs.
*   Duplication is avoided, and economies of scale are achieved in various specialties.
*   Simplicity with clear assignments for each department.
*   Accountability is easy to track.

### Disadvantages

*   Encourages empire building and managers may not relate to or support objectives of other functional areas.

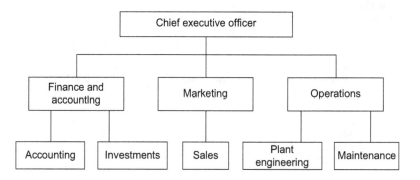

*Figure 4.1* Functional organisational structure

- Easier to lose sight of customers, as employees focus on their area of specialisation.
- Creates barriers to coordination and communication among units, as each develops its own language or jargon, reward systems and sub-culture.
- Does not encourage early development of general management talent, because the focus is specialisation.
- As size increases, this structure may be less appropriate.

### *Product Structure*

Product structures focus on products and groups jobs and activities associated with a particular product. The product manager is responsible for many or all aspects of a product or product line. In its pure form, this structure creates several smaller, single product-line units, each with its functional specialties. Often, however, a product manager has responsibility only for marketing and sales and relies on other managers for services including cost control, product quality and product delivery. This is a hybrid of the product and functional structures. Product structures emphasise the importance of the firm's products by holding the product manager accountable for the profitability of the product line. An example is given in Figure 4.2.

### Advantages of the Product Structure

- Combines a product focus with the benefits of functional specialisation at a lower level.

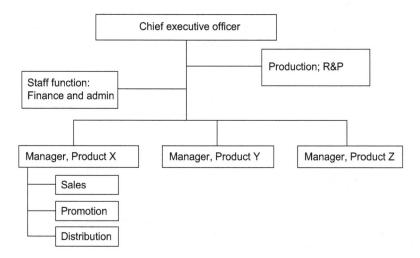

*Figure 4.2* Product structure

- High-performing people and other resources can focus on demanding products and devote less attention to poorly performing ones.
- Effective training for general managers because product managers make decisions and manage across functions.
- Fosters greater concern for long-term issues, relating to product line development.

**Disadvantages**

- More costly because of duplication of resources and functional specialists for each product/product line.
- Smaller, less successful product-oriented functional departments may not pay attention to skill development, because of inadequate resources for staff development.
- Tight corporate control on profits may result in tight product line controls limiting risk-taking, adaptability and innovation.
- Barriers to communication and coordination grow because each product manager is paid and encouraged to focus on her/his product and not others.

### *Matrix Structure*

The matrix structure combines different types of designs; for example, a project (organised around individual projects) and functional design (see Figure 4.3), and there are two or more lines of authority; for example a functional line with managers heading functional areas such as manufacturing,

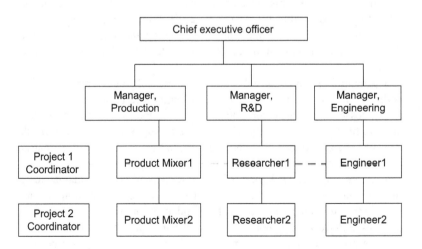

*Figure 4.3* Matrix structure

marketing or finance, the other project managers, charged with the budget for a project. Functional managers (e.g. Head of Manufacturing) have the staff with competencies under them but no budget, while project managers have money but no staff. They have to work together to get the project completed; functional managers have to release staff to work on a project and project managers have to release money. The functional employee will have more than one superior, the project manager and the functional manager, with each having influence on employee performance. The functional manager pays the salary and the project manager contributes to performance review since she or he sees his or her work across a number of projects. The dual authority structure of the matrix permits focus on project efficiency while maintaining the specialist development of the functional structure—which ensures functional resources are available when needed.

The matrix structure requires special management and employee skills. High levels of trust, communication, negotiation, teamwork, ability to shift focus and priority and attention to detail are essential to managing and working in a matrix. Managers and employees need training to make decisions based on expertise, persuasion and logic, rather than hierarchical position and formal roles; misunderstandings, disagreements and conflicts must be dealt with through confrontation and problem solving, rather than appeals to higher authority. The general atmosphere of the matrix firm is to emphasise task contribution and accomplishments above personal rank and status.

Matrix structures are useful for projects, with a clear beginning and end, such as building a bridge or dam. It is used for complex tasks, including designing, and building large items (e.g. airplanes, ships) or when moving to a new plant site. This structure balances project and technical goals, allocating responsibility for both. It is used for mergers and acquisitions, and where resources are limited and there is high and temporary resource demand, coupled with high levels of complexity and uncertainty in a project.

The main disadvantages of the matrix include lack of clear responsibility, authority and jurisdiction. The 'matrixed' employee typically has two or more 'bosses' and must determine whom to listen to when. This often creates confusion and ambiguity. These concerns suggest a matrix can result in some chaos and disorder, and may engender power struggles. Matrix structures may encourage cliques since decisions are made by a group. This creates loyalties and potential inter-group conflicts. The maintenance of two management hierarchies is expensive, and the costs of training and maintaining this interpersonal, skill-dependent form are significant. Managers used to working in more traditional strictures may find it hard to operate contrary to the unity of command principle, which requires one-person/one-boss and a clear line-of-authority.

## Customer Structure

Customer structures focus on customer needs rather than functional skills, product brands or projects. Activities and positions are grouped in terms of special needs of specific customers; often in service-oriented industries (e.g. an investment firm with one group devoted to high-wealth individuals, another to pension plans, another to small investors etc.). Customer segmentation is also used in sales departments offering different terms to different kinds of customers (e.g. volume discounts to large customers). The customer structure shows that management is sensitive to customers' needs and have identified segments with special requirements.

The advantage of this structure is that it focuses where revenue is generated. Companies differentiated by customer type are often sophisticated in understanding and meeting the needs of their customers. The disadvantage is pressure to meet varying customers' demands, leading to complexities in production/service scheduling and shorter production runs, which are expensive.

## Geographical Structure

Geographical structures group activities and positions at a physical location to take advantage of local participation in decision-making. The geographical structure may contain a functional structure. For example, TANESCO, Tanzania's only electricity company has a regional structure, with each independent region having functional roles such as marketing, finance and so on. The geographical structure reflects decentralisation. The territorial units are under the control of a manager who is responsible for all operations at a particular location.

This structure is used where a company has subsidiaries in other countries, and many 'regional divisions' are countries, each with their own cultural, legal, financial and managerial parameters. International companies also use regional groupings, such as North America, Central America and the Caribbean, North Africa, Sub-Saharan Africa and so on.

Most divisions of this type are based on geography as described but distance may not be the only reason for a geographic form. Other factors might be used, such as level of economic development or political system. Changes in the legal environment, cultural norms and topography may be factors. Student projects (the University of Dar es Salaam) showed most large companies, privately and publicly owned, with operations in regions away from headquarters, had adopted regional structures. For example:

The National Health Insurance Fund has nine zonal (regional) offices across the country, reporting to head office. There are also four directorates, three are line directorates: Benefits and Administration, Field Operation, Planning and Actuarial Services; one is staff, Finance and Human Resources. Other supporting offices/units are internal audit, procurement, legal services and communication.

(Godi, 2009)

### *Divisional Structure*

This involves a multiproduct or service design that separates different products or services to facilitate planning and control (see Figure 4.4). A large organisation such as Dangote Group from Nigeria with very varied product lines (ranging from cement, to sugar, salt, flour, pasta, beverages and real estate and, expanding into the oil and gas, petrochemicals, fertilisers and agriculture) may consider this structure. This structure is also denoted as M-Form (Ouchi, 1984). Different divisions in the organisation can have simple centralised or functional designs, depending on their size and activities. This design is favoured when different kinds of products or services require different kinds of management. The divisional structure may be considered an extension of the product form but with much greater responsibility and scope of control for the general manager. An individual is placed in charge of a 'business', defined by product group, location or clusters of products. Divisions typically are responsible for their own business from start to finish, including financing, raw materials, manufacturing, sales, and marketing and so on.

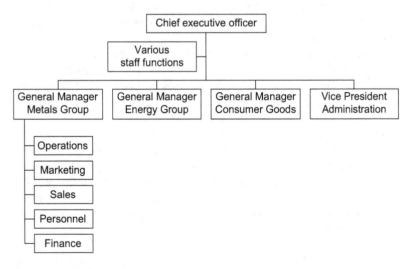

*Figure 4.4* Divisional form

*Source*: Pitts and Clawson (2000).

They may have authority to organise their divisions as appropriate, given that different businesses face different environments. Some may be considered 'profit centres' if they have control over revenues and costs, so their profits can be calculated and evaluated as they would be in a stand-alone business.

Ouchi (1984) argued that the M-form strikes a balance between independence and interdependence among organisational units. He believed an organisation should not have units completely dependent on each other as in the functional form or totally independent like the product form. By striking a balance, organisational units can maximise profits and still share in the allocation of common expenses from divisions. All units are interdependent through shared resources. The formal structure of the divisional form reflects the tension between dependence and independence in organisations and provides a means to attain a balance between autonomy for the division and central control for the corporation. The disadvantage of the M-form is its complexity, which requires experience and judgement to be effective. It can lead to redundancies and sometimes breakdowns in service to the consumer. The M-form creates needs for careful and thoughtful integration systems and mechanisms.

### *Adhocratic/Amorphous Structures*

These are also called 'free form' or organic structures that stress managerial styles and do not depend on formal structures. Individual managers develop the organisation they need to accomplish their purposes. Organic systems reflect senior management trust in middle managers or apathy towards structure. They are suited to complex and non-standard work that need informal structures. 'Organic' or 'amorphous' forms seem to be gaining in popularity among high-tech companies, during the growth of the information age. The emergence of so-called virtual organisations where most functions of traditional organisations are sub-contracted also complicates the current panorama of structural alternatives (Pitts & Clawson, 2000). In addition, the COVID pandemic has encouraged virtual work, and to the extent this has been successful, there is likely to be more in the future.

An adhocratic structure is flexible, adaptive and organised around special problems to be solved by a group consisting of experts with diverse professional skills. These experts have decision-making authority and other powers, with an ill defined hierarchy. This design works for high technology and high growth organisations where an arranged and inflexible structure may be a handicap. New theories of network organisations are emerging and influencing design decisions.

Pitts and Clawson (2000) believe organic structures have the potential for providing a highly motivating environment for achievement-oriented, internally motivated individuals. With the right kind of talent, they can respond quickly to environmental or technological changes. Organic structures are used by entrepreneurs, focused on rapid growth, who believe too much structure is stifling or do not have time to pay attention to the challenges of organising. The downside is that they can become tangles of confused, undirected effort, producing little more than friction and heat. To be successful, recruiting systems must select only those who fit the needs of the organisation and can function in such a structure. Uncontrolled growth can be expensive and even fatal with little or no structure.

### Other Structures

Hybrid structures combine different forms to produce a mixed one, such as the matrix. The idea is to combine different forms, capitalising on advantages and minimising disadvantages. Finally, organisational structures may be created around processes, equipment, time of duty, number of employees, markets, distribution channels and so on. For example, a machine department may be created by grouping jobs and activities related to different machines.

## Considerations Relevant to the African Context

The discussion so far has been about organisational structures of formal organisations. These include multinational companies, state-owned enterprises and similar organisations that are likely to adopt one of or a combination of the structures discussed. In the African context, most businesses are small, family-owned, with simple functional structures. These organisations, where owner/managers have a few employees reporting to her or him and where more informal ways (versus formal, written and procedure-based) are likely to be prevalent still need to be organised. In informal businesses, however, such as those owned and run by *mama ntilie* or *baba ntilie* (food vendors run by women or men), kiosks, small groceries, small tailoring businesses, small pharmacies and shops, there may be no formal structure at all, as the owner is usually the manager and staff of such one-person owned/run businesses. Concepts about organisational design may therefore apply only to a limited extent in these settings.

## Conclusion

We discussed organisational structures, explaining that organising involves defining activities and grouping them to form units/departments, assigning activities to people, and showing relationships between departments. Various forms of organisational structures were presented and their advantages and disadvantages outlined. Organisations may use one structure or combine different structures to achieve an optimal structure for the business. Organisational structures are not static and businesses and other organisations change their structures in response to technology, organisation growth and the external environment. The underlying idea is to have a structure that supports and enables the organisation to achieve its goals. Changes in the organisational structure may occur incrementally or drastically depending on factors motivating the change and management's response to these changes. In the African context, organisational structures will be adapted to the operating business situations.

## Review/Discussion

1. Explain the term organising.
2. Describe what is meant by an organisational structure.
3. Describe the principles underpinning organisational structures.
4. Discuss the difference between unity of command and span of control.
5. Discuss the following. 'The cultural values of African people are such that older people have to be respected and held in high regard by younger ones. In situations where a younger person has more technical expertise, and hence qualifies to be in a higher position than an older person, how can organisational structures be designed to avoid tensions that may occur if the younger person is the boss of the older person?'

## Exercise

Tanzania Breweries Limited (TBL), a member of the Anheuser-Busch InBev group of companies, manufactures, sells and distributes clear beer, alcoholic fruit beverages and non-alcoholic beverages within Tanzania. TBL, as a major player in the beverage sector, is committed to the export of its products to niche and neighbouring markets under the East Africa Common Market trading arrangement. TBL has a controlling interest in Tanzania Distilleries Limited, Darbrew Limited and Kibo Breweries Limited. The Management of the Company is under the Managing Director and is organised in the following departments: Supply Chain Department, Logistics Department, Solutions Department, Finance Department; Marketing Department, Sales Department, People Department and Corporate Affairs and Legal Department'. Source (Tanzania Breweries Limited (TBL) pp. 3, 16)

> *Question:* What form of organisational structure do you think TBL has adopted? Explain your answer.

> **Assignment:** Download annual reports of three listed companies and review their statements on how the company is organised. Explain, based on this chapter, how the companies are organised. Discuss your findings with your colleagues.

# References

Fayol, H. (1949). *General and Industrial Management*. Translated by C. Storrs. London: Pitman.

Godi, G. (2009). Effectiveness of Managerial Budgetary Control in Social Health Insurance Organizations: A case study of National Health Insurance Fund in Tanzania, MBA Dissertation, University of Dar es Salaam.

Ouchi, W. G. (1984). *The M-Form Society*. New York: Avon.

Pitts, T., & Clawson, J. B. (2000). *Organisational Structure: A Technical Note*. Charlottesville, VA: University of Virginia Darden Foundation.

Taylor, F. W. (1947). *Principles of Scientific Management*. New York, NY: Harper.

Weber, M. (1947). *The Theory of Social and Economic Organisation*. Translated by T. Parsons. New York, NY: Free Press.

# 5 Staffing

## Chapter Summary

The third management function is staffing. Staffing involves filling positions in an organisation and ensuring that people in those positions can and do carry out the work that is required for the organisation to continue and succeed. We consider staffing activities including how they apply to Africa. We also briefly outline labour relations issues.

---

### Learning Outcomes

After completing this chapter, you will be able to:

- Describe the activities involved in staffing.
- Explain the difference between personnel management and human resource management.
- Define strategic human resource management.
- Discuss various aspects of staffing, including recruiting, hiring, training, evaluation, careers and dismissal and how they occur in African countries.
- Identify and discuss aspects of the African context in terms of human resource decisions.

---

## Introduction

In the west, up to the 1950s, what is now called HRM was often called personnel management (PM), and was a relatively simple administrative function of attracting, hiring, training, implementing management's instructions on dismissing employees and keeping records of personnel, including attendance, vacations, pay, bonuses, pensions and the like. PM departments

DOI: 10.4324/9781003017516-5

were responsible for the paperwork associated with having employees. After the 1950s, there was an argument that 'managing personnel' should involve much more, and PM was expanded to include issues such as motivation, leadership, performance, employee/management development and career management. HR departments became responsible for ensuring the overall effective management of people in organisations, built on the idea that people are the organisation's most valuable resource. Today, many argue that HRM should be strategic in nature and that the function should be called strategic human resource management (SHRM). In this view, the HRM function is closely tied into the strategic direction of the organisation, because employees provide vital and valuable inputs into strategic achievement. SHRM means decisions about human resources are made in the context of strategy and strategy is influenced by human resource issues. More recently, the term talent management has become common as organisations seek to identify those with talent who can help achieve strategic goals. HRM, in a formal sense, is often largely non-existent in small and family-owned firms, and for these companies this probably works quite well, because human resource decisions are made informally and based on personal knowledge. Even in these organisations it is a good idea for managers to understand the fundamentals of HRM and use those approaches that may help them manage their human resources more effectively.

In the next section, the nature of the human resource function in African countries is examined, followed by discussion of aspects of staffing, including hiring, training, dismissal, career management, retirement and so on. The role of labour relations is also briefly presented.

## Human Resource Management in the African Context

Budhwar and Debrah (2001) examined HRM in developing countries and their analysis is appropriate to the African context. They suggested that HRM was influenced by three sets of factors: national factors including (1) national culture, institutions, business sectors and the dynamic business environment; (2) contingent factors including age, size, nature, ownership, life-cycle stage, trade unions, HR strategies and stakeholder interests and (3) organisational strategies and policies related to primary HR functions and internal labour markets. They noted that 'HRM in developing countries is in its infancy' (p. 6).

Budhwar and Debrah said 'in almost all of the countries, personnel management (PM) and HRM are used interchangeably but often implying a bureaucratic PM system' (p. 249). It is likely this is the case in much of Africa. This is hardly surprising, given that richer countries have only moved to a more proactive human resource approach in the past 50 years and that the concept of SHRM is still in its infancy. Further, they said that globalisation, and the instability and uncertainty that developing countries face, make it imperative that they establish appropriate approaches for managing human resources. This is an area where African organisations can learn from the experience of their western counterparts by adopting HRM and SHRM practices and focusing on talent management. Previously, we noted that African countries have large young populations, high youth unemployment and relatively low levels of educational attainment. These characteristics underscore the need to pay attention to the HR function by instituting effective policies that take these characteristics into account.

Budhwar and Debrah noted the major influence of religion and traditional cultural beliefs on HRM practices. These are clearly relevant in the African context. We have mentioned Ubuntu in other chapters, and it would seem that a belief that 'I am because we are' would be a good foundation for effective HR, allowing the use of individual talent for the benefit of the whole. We have, however, also outlined a culture of what is sometimes termed '*tribal loyalty*' in African countries, and this can have a negative impact on HR practices, by favouring one group over others, and creating an 'in-group/out-group' mentality which impedes performance. The question of how the youths are valued is also relevant to HRM. If they are seen as providing an innovative, motivated and productive workforce, HRM will seek to make the most of these employees. In contrast, if they are undisciplined, unmotivated and unproductive, HR policies may focus on constraining and holding them in check. In general terms, the United Nation's Office of the Special Advisor on Africa says that effective policies and measures are critical to harness the benefits of the potential youth demographic dividend. This is equally the case in organisations where effective HRM policies and measures can ensure the youthful population is treated as a benefit.

## Staffing Activities

Next we consider basic staffing activities—recruiting, hiring, training, career planning, dismissal and retirement. These occur in some form in all organisations to ensure a complement of staff that performs so the company functions reasonably well, or preferably at a high level, and continues to operate. The way companies carry out these activities differs, however, because of conditions; for example, in small-/medium-sized companies, staffing may be relatively informal while in larger organisations activities are formal and possibly bureaucratic, with detailed administrative procedures. In Africa, there are many micro-enterprises, many family-owned companies or ones owned by a small group of close associates, many engaged in basic agricultural processing, assembly work or relatively simple manufacturing, requiring relatively low-skill employees. In these companies, we expect informal staffing practices; for example, when hiring a new employee, the manager(s)/owners may simply let it be known and current employees may suggest someone (often a relative) to fill the position. Interestingly, however, a study in Sierra Leone found a significant positive relationship between HRM practices and SME performance, including sales. The author concluded that SMEs are at a disadvantage relative to larger companies in terms of their staffing, and that more formal HR practices could help them become more competitive (Kanu, 2015).

### *Recruiting*

To staff an organisation, one has to find appropriate people for positions that need to be filled. There are many ways to recruit people for jobs; ranging from informal to formal. At the informal extreme, a company uses word of mouth and networking—letting people know that a job is available and needs to be filled, or asking current employees, relatives, friends or neighbours to suggest someone. At the formal extreme, a company hires a professional search firm to advertise the position, identify and screen potential candidates, check references and provide recommendations on suitable candidates. In-between, companies can advertise positions in various media, review applicants for other positions, go to job fairs at schools and universities and get lists of applicants from employment agencies.

The recruitment process depends on characteristics of the position to be filled, the company and industry and the country in which the position exists:

- The more important the position and the larger the company, the more extensive and formal the search is likely be. Top-level positions such as chief executive officer or chairman of the board are not usually publicised and there are firms that specialise in finding candidates for these positions, often based on knowledge about individuals who may consider changing positions (i.e. 'head-hunting').
- The characteristics of the industry influence the nature of the search because of the specialised skills and experience that may be required in a particular industry. The more specialised the skills needed the more extensive and formal the search will be.
- The norms and expectations in a particular country affect formality and the media used for recruitment. Where formality is usual, companies will be relatively formal, and vice versa. If job fairs are held regularly, they will be used, if newspapers are read regularly, they will be used, where the internet is common, it will be favoured and so on.

The Internet and various social networks are now commonly used to recruit new hires. For example, the LinkedIn network in North America was promoted as an employment networking site. It is also common for recruiters to check potential employees' personal websites and pages, because these provide information not likely to be included on a resume or volunteered during an interview.

The nature of business in African countries suggests that many companies will use informal methods for recruiting new employees. In family-owned firms, family members are recruited for important jobs, as they are considered more trustworthy than outsiders and their skills and abilities are well known, so there is no need for a formal recruitment process. For lower level positions, family 'retainers' (people who have worked with the family in various roles for many years) and their families are often preferred. They are known and expected to be loyal, and it is expected that owners look after them by providing employment. Alternatively, the friends and family of current employees are seen as preferable to strangers, even where the strangers may be more educated or skilled.

In the west, and in developed countries generally, hiring close relatives and friends is called nepotism and is seen as negative, and in some companies, close relatives are not allowed to work in the same department. The common belief is that one cannot be objective about family and friends and will favour them. The reverse is true in many developing countries, where the belief is that family and friends will work hard and they can be trusted, so hiring them is seen as positive. Similarly, in small, family-run firms in more developed countries, family members are usually in key positions.

The HR literature suggests that a key evolution, if small and family firms are to grow, is the transition from family management to management based on skills, experience and expertise. Companies in African countries should consider the more formal options available for the selection process, particularly as they grow. A more formal process is likely to give the company access to a wider range of candidates, and candidates with better skills and experience for a particular position. Family members and friends do not necessarily have the needed skills, they may not be interested in a particular job, and they may not always be trustworthy or hard working.

### *Hiring*

Hiring processes also range from informal to formal. At the informal end, decision makers discuss possible candidates and make a decision, then offer the person a job, and acceptance is likely, because wages and benefits do not vary a lot, and good jobs may be scarce. At the formal end, candidates are evaluated using a variety of assessment instruments, focusing on skills and psychological attributes; candidates go through a rigorous screening, interviewing and reference checking process; each candidate is assessed on merit and against other candidates. Offers are made to desirable candidates and salary and benefits negotiated, before a final hiring decision is made.

If the selection process is informal, the hiring process is likely to be informal. The candidates being considered are probably well known, implying that rigorous assessment is not needed. A formal process can take time and may be seen as costly. In smaller, family-run firms, where a position needs to be filled there may be some time pressure, and additional costs have to be clearly justified. Owners and managers may not be familiar with more formal techniques, so they may not even consider a more formal approach. How well someone will fit into the existing organisation is probably seen as more important than specific skills or psychological attributes. Interviewing is also likely to be informal and may not even take place in many situations.

While the norm in hiring may be informal, this does not mean that it is always best. For jobs requiring particular skills and attributes, it is appropriate to apply formal approaches. Testing potential employees, in-depth interviews with a variety of managers and employees, and reference checking can go a long way to ensuring a good fit between the person hired, the position and the company. A challenge for African companies is that many of the available assessment instruments have not been designed with Africa in mind. HR managers may need to test a variety of instruments to identify those that seem to be effective for their needs. More formal approaches seem time-consuming and costly, but they can save time and costs associated with training, help ensure new employees are productive quickly and should lower turnover and the need to dismiss new hires.

Specific HR 'best practices' may need to be adjusted because of local values. Cunningham and Rowley (2007) found that interviews were not seen favourably in China, where personal networks are very important and Akorsu (2010) argued that typical HR practices from developed countries do not work in the informal economy of Ghana. The informal economy is a particular sector that is quite different from the formal economy—jobs are low-paying, without contracts, often on a day-to-day basis. Under these conditions, Akorsu found recruitment and selection were done on the basis of personal contacts and humanitarian grounds, performance was not formally evaluated and benefits were not offered. This seemed to work well because apprenticeships were common and the relationship between employer and apprentice was close.

## *Training*

Training in most African small businesses is sometimes seen as a 'frill'— nice to have, but not necessary. Training costs are immediate and obvious, while benefits are longer term and not easily quantifiable, particularly for nontechnical training and development. Technical training that is required to perform a specific job may be a necessity. Nontechnical training, such as communication, conflict resolution, team building and so on may not seem to provide concrete cost–benefit advantages.

In African countries, financial resources are limited and it may be difficult to devote limited resources to training. Training to do a particular job is necessary, but if relatively low skill, co-workers can be responsible for training new employees to perform required tasks. For example, in the informal sector in Ghana, training was done through the apprenticeship system, minimising training expenditures. In such situations, developmental training may seem a waste of financial resources.

It is understandable that companies devote relatively little of limited financial resources to training, but this may be short-sighted. As African companies compete more and more with counterparts from developed countries, both at home and in foreign markets, training and development of employees and managers may provide the competitive advantage to succeed in a global environment. African organisations need to identify the training and development needs that are specific to them and build programmes that are appropriate to these specific needs. Training is one area where cultural differences are likely to have an impact on effectiveness; therefore, designing culturally appropriate training programs is critical. For example, in Africa:

- somewhat collective cultures—training will likely need to be done for groups or teams working closely together;
- somewhat high on uncertainty avoidance—training will likely need to be structured, with correct responses clearly identified;
- somewhat high on power—distance—training that is introduced and supported by those at higher levels are likely to be accepted, and trainers should be in positions of power.

### Performance Evaluation

Evaluating performance in Western literature is considered a critical aspect of managing people. Evaluating performance allows employees to understand the areas where they perform well, and where they need to improve. This improves individual performance and ensures that the organisation performs at a high level.

In African countries, performance evaluation may be seen as less important because:

- Employees may be at low levels; therefore, evaluation is at a basic level—for example, did the employee produce the required number of units? Did the employee visit the required sites? In this case, there is little consideration of how performance affects progression through the organisation instead it becomes an assessment of whether the organisation should keep the employee.

- Employees may be employed on a 'day labourer' basis—only when there is work available. This makes formal performance evaluation more short-term oriented.
- Employees may be family members, and the formal evaluation of family members does not work effectively. Family members are expected to participate in the organisation, so evaluation seems to be irrelevant, because they will be employed/retained regardless of performance.
- Performance evaluation requires specification of targets and monitoring of actual performance relative to targets. Many small companies do not collect data on a regular basis and have only an informal idea of what levels of performance are possible or desirable.

While formal performance evaluation can seem unimportant, evaluation can have a positive effect on performance in all companies. Having a clear understanding of what is expected in terms of performance, and actual performance relative to this standard, allows employees to reach expected levels and adjust work habits if they are not reaching these. In many African countries where people may be working for basic levels of pay, and want to avoid uncertainty, knowing clearly what is expected and how well they are performing relative to expectations, provides a degree of certainty that can be motivating.

The way performance evaluation is carried out needs to fit the cultural characteristics of the particular country/organisation. Some examples of culturally contingent evaluation:

- If the country is relatively high on collectivism, then performance targets as well as evaluation probably work best when they are group based. Singling out an individual, even for good performance, may have negative consequences in collective countries. In contrast, in individualistic countries, performance targets that are individually determined are effective, and evaluation is done on a person-by-person basis, and individuals are often singled out publicly for good performance.
- If a country is high on power distance, then the performance targets can be set by the supervisors and managers for those at lower levels, and this will probably be more acceptable than participative setting of performance levels. In contrast, in low power—distance countries, participation in setting of performance targets is often considered critical to acceptance of these targets; in these countries, managers and

employees usually review actual performance together and mutually agree on how well employees have performed, and if remedial action is needed.

- In more masculine countries (societies that hold traditional male values), performance is likely to be tied to tangible rewards, including pay increases and prizes, such as holidays, household goods, cars and so on, and competition for these rewards can be an effective inducement to perform at a high level. In more feminine countries (societies that hold traditional female values), cooperation is likely to be favoured over competition, and rewards are more likely to be time off, or social events that encourage interaction among group members.

- In countries where uncertainty avoidance is high, performance targets need to be specific and as concrete as possible, so it is clear to employees exactly what is expected of them. Evaluation can then be clearly related to the expected performance, with criteria that do not leave room for questions about performance levels. Performance levels in turn should be clearly related to outcomes such as bonuses or other rewards. Where improvements in performance are needed, these should also be clearly specified to avoid any uncertainty. In countries where uncertainty avoidance is low, people may be comfortable with relatively open-ended performance targets and measures, as they feel that this gives them more leeway to adjust to a changing environment and still perform well.

- In countries with a longer time horizon, performance evaluation may be done at relatively long intervals, based on long-term goals. In countries with a shorter time horizon, performance targets will need to be shorter term, and long-term goals need to be broken down into near-term objectives, so that performance can be monitored and evaluated at frequent intervals.

A small, family-owned company can keep performance evaluation relatively informal. There may be no need to design and implement complex systems, in fact, these can do more harm than good, if employees do not see the need for them. Some performance evaluation, nevertheless, is needed to ensure that both managers and employees know what performance is expected and how well people are performing relative to expectations.

### *Career Planning*

The concept of career planning in organisations may be virtually non-existent in many African countries. In fact, the concept of a career is somewhat meaningless, as many people simply work in order to make enough money to live, and in some countries employees work until they have enough money 'for the time being' then don't come to work for a while. The distinction between management and employees is clear-cut and there is little expectation that employees will move to management levels. Many companies are small and family-owned with management made up of family members, friends and perhaps a few carefully selected, trusted outsiders. If career planning is considered, it is often in the context of the expected progression of family members. Family members may start at the bottom of the organisation in to learn all aspects of operations, but they are expected to progress through the organisation relatively quickly to the management level. Particular family members may be identified to eventually become the president/chief executive officer/managing director and these family members will be singled out for special training and development to ensure that they can take on this role.

Career planning, insofar as it exists is likely to be informal. Trusted individuals who perform well at lower levels may be identified as having management potential, and these individuals will then receive special treatment and encouragement to help them achieve this potential. The issue of trust tends to be as important as ability and potential. The nature of small firms, especially family-owned ones, is that being able to trust people in management positions is seen as essential. Trust may be based on relationships beyond the enterprise and extend to personal, intra-family relationships.

Career planning may contribute positively to performance. Pacek and Thorniley (2004) found that career planning was an important aspect of job satisfaction, and job satisfaction has been shown to relate to positive job results such as performance and productivity, as well as negative results, such as absenteeism, tardiness and turnover. Companies in Africa should consider instituting some formal career planning to allow employees to see their jobs as more than simply a series of days of going to work. Of course, issues of culture should be considered, so, for example, in collective cultures career planning may be for a team or group of employees.

As companies grow, and increasingly become international, career planning is a necessity. Larger companies cannot rely only on family members and close associates. They need to develop a professional management group. Once a company moves to a professional management approach, issues of ability become particularly relevant. These companies find that formal career planning is essential to identifying and developing managers and executives. At the same time, corporate growth implies more levels within the organisation and more specialisation of functions, hence opportunity for employees to progress up the hierarchy.

*Dismissal*

Where employees do not perform at acceptable levels, or where their behaviour is unacceptable (e.g. they are frequently late or absent, they do not work well with others, they are abusive to colleagues etc.), it becomes necessary to dismiss them. Where labour laws are well established, these specify the actions necessary for dismissal. These usually include giving verbal and written warnings, keeping written documentation of performance and any incidents that may lead to dismissal, as well as the timeframe that is required for dismissal to take effect, and the monetary settlement that is required. Individual companies often have their own policies as well. While these must comply with the law, they often go further, especially where strong unions are present.

In countries where labour laws are less well established, dismissal may be relatively easy. It may be possible to dismiss someone on the spot for a perceived infraction or lack of performance, or even without any specific reason. Where employees are not employed on a continuing basis, but on a daily basis, and they are paid on a daily basis; dismissal is simply a matter of telling the employee that they will not be needed in the future, and paying whatever is owed at that point in time. Of course, where unions or similar groups are present, and relatively strong, they may seek redress, even where employees are employed in a daily basis, so unions will be a factor in dismissal decisions.

In some cultures, employers are seen as having obligations to their employees and their families, and these obligations continue even when an employee is not performing at expected levels. In these countries, employers may continue to employ people who are not contributing, and may 'make' work for these employees where there really is no work. In Japan it has been typical for employees to have a job for life, so once hired, it was unlikely you would be made redundant or dismissed. In China, the communist tradition in state-owned enterprises was known as the 'Iron Rice Bowl', where employees were guaranteed a job, a place to live and so on, as well as a certain wage, regardless of the organisation's needs or the person's performance.

## Labour Relations

Labour relations vary substantially across countries. In some locations, the concept of labour unions, and labour—management negotiations and agreements, is in the early formation stages. Akorsu (2010) asked workers in the informal sector in Ghana about trade unions, and got the answer essentially 'what are trade unions?' At the other extreme, in some developing countries, labour—management relations are antagonistic and the labour movement adversarial, with a union activist labour environment that is influential in government policy and decision-making. Unions in the developing world have often formed because of the power of the collectivism of trade unions, and the leaders of unions became the political leaders during the struggles for independence and afterwards.

We cannot generalise about labour–management relations. Each country has to be understood in its own context. The strength of the union movement and unions varies with a country's commitment to the supremacy of law in the society. Budhwar and Debrah (2001) concluded that almost all countries have legal structures to safeguard the interests of employees, but often they are not enforced, and many countries do not promote equal opportunities based on factors such as ethnicity, gender and age. They also noted that unions developed confrontational attitudes which served them well during independence struggles, but that these may do more harm than good in today's world. They suggested that where there is a cooperative labour—management environment, and the role of governments in unions is curtailed, this will be beneficial.

## Conclusion

This chapter examined aspects of HRM from an African perspective. The HRM field seems to be relatively under-developed in many countries and reasons for this were explored. The characteristics of many African companies may argue against formal HRM; nevertheless, companies can learn from the practices that have been found effective in other countries where HRM is more formal and strategic.

## Review/Discussion

1.  Discuss what you believe are the most important HRM challenges facing African countries. What are the most important issues relating to HRM in your country?
2.  'In a small, African country, HR systems are unnecessary'. Discuss the pros and cons of this statement.
3.  Identify the main cultural characteristics of a specific African country and discuss how these characteristics are likely to impact on HRM practices.
4.  Select an organisation, in your country, and evaluate its HR systems. What do you think is positive about the system? What needs to be changed and in what way? How has this company, firm or organisation aligned its HRM practices with its strategy?

## Exercise

A medium-sized company located in sub-Saharan Africa has decided to expand to markets in North America. Following analysis, the company has chosen to concentrate on Canada for its first foray into exports to North America. The company has advertised on the internet and in local newspapers for someone to spearhead the 'Canadian Export Development' venture. It has received responses, some of which were surprising, because they came from outside of Africa. The company has identified three that it believes are the best. Following is a brief biography of these three.

1.  Mary Jane Smith is 40 years old and holds an MBA in export marketing and speaks English and French fluently. She is a Canadian citizen and has worked in the marketing areas of several large companies in Canada. She thinks this is an exciting opportunity and looks forward to the challenge. She has visited Africa (Egypt and Morocco) in the past, and enjoyed these experiences.
2.  Joshua Nkomo is 35 years old and has a BA in marketing. He is a Nigerian citizen and has worked in Nigeria and in Europe. He believes his knowledge of Africa and Europe will allow him to address the Canadian export market from a positive perspective. He has visited Toronto in Canada once, and has cousins who live there.
3.  Sadima Solo is 30 years old, has a BA in languages and speaks several languages fluently. She has dual citizenship in Ghana and Canada and has lived in both countries. She thinks it is fantastic that this position would allow her to use her knowledge of both Africa and Canada to benefit an African company. She loves travelling and believes this position provides great opportunities.

Based on this very limited information, how would you evaluate each candidate? What do you see as positive? What do you see as negative? What additional information would you want in order to make a selection? If you had to make a decision based on the limited information, which candidate would you choose? Why?

## References

Akorsu, A. D. (2010). Labour management practices in the informal economy of Ghana: A deviation from the HRM orthodoxy? Presented at *International Symposium on Human Resource Management in Africa*. Nottingham, U.K.: Nottingham Trent University, September.

Budhwar, P. S., & Debrah, Y. A. (2001). *Human Resources in Developing Countries*. London: Routledge.

Cunningham, L. X., & Rowley, C. (2007). Human resource management in Chinese small and medium enterprises: A review and research agenda. *Personnel Review*, 36(3), 415–439.

Kanu, A. M. (2015). An investigation into the prevalence of HRM practices in SMEs: Sierra Leone an example. *Developing Country Studies*, 5(6).

Pacek, N., & Thorniley, D. (2004). *Emerging Markets: Lessons for Business Success and the Outlook for Different Markets*. London: The Economist with Profile Books.

# 6 Directing

## Chapter Summary

The fourth management function, directing, is primarily concerned with the people side of management. Directing ensures employees are willing to perform to achieve the organisation's goals, contribute to its strategy and conform to its culture. Directing encompasses leadership and motivation. In this chapter, we discuss related theories and argue that they are essentially universal although context influences the way effective leadership and motivation are achieved. We consider the African context to illustrate how this occurs.

---

### Learning Outcomes

After completing this chapter, you will be able to:

- Explain the general concepts of leadership and motivation.
- Present leadership theories.
- Explain concepts of leadership in the African context.
- Discuss different theories of motivation.
- Describe the process of leading and motivating employees.
- Explain the different characteristics of African countries and how they may affect leadership and motivation.

---

## Leadership and Motivation

There are many definitions of leadership. We define it as a process of influence where the leader enlists the aid and support of others to accomplish common tasks. Leadership involves people and tasks and followers as well as a leader. There may be more than one leader and, sometimes only one follower. There may be one task or many. Leaders also play different roles. There may be formal leaders and informal ones; there may be task leaders and social leaders.

DOI: 10.4324/9781003017516-6

Leadership is closely linked to motivation because leaders motivate followers to behave in desired ways. Motivation is the reason(s) people act/behave in particular ways. Motivation is the underlying force that impels us to do things. Punnett (2019) states that motivation is a universal concept—people everywhere have needs and wants that are the basis on which they will act—however, what motivates, when and where will differ depending on the society and culture as well as the individual.

Following, we expand on these concepts and explain various theories, considering how various characteristics of African countries may affect leadership and motivation.

## Importance of Leadership

Leadership is a critical aspect of management. Getting others to work towards a common goal is key to an organisation's success. Effective leadership is needed by for-profit and not-for-profit organisations to fulfil their missions. Without leadership, organisations can move slowly, stagnate or lose their way. Management literature ties organisational success to decisions and strategy. A well-crafted strategy is not meaningful unless implemented. This requires leadership. Effective leadership helps organisations through times of difficulty, building cohesion to achieve outcomes that everybody appreciates at the workplace. Given the importance of effective leadership, we ask what makes an effective leader? Is it some physical trait of the leader (e.g. being tall or attractive?); personality (e.g. emotional intelligence?); relationship between leaders and followers (e.g. guiding and coaching); focusing on productivity and the task; the cultural environment (e.g. a view of power or individualism?). Understanding what makes an effective leader is complex and depends on many factors, probably encompassing all of the above.

There is overlap between management and leadership, but the two concepts are different. There are leaders who are not managers; there are managers who are not leaders. Leaders have people who follow them while managers are in positions where people work for them. They are responsible for people producing at a certain level, have control over resources and have the authority to enforce policies/procedures, rules/regulations, which help control subordinates. Managers may achieve desired/required production levels through resources, policies, rules and so on, while a leader has people who want to act in accord with the leader's vision and because of the leader's characteristics.

As an example: Ms. Ocechuku is a manager of a sales department for a shoe manufacturer. She is responsible for assigning sales territories and targets to salespeople. The salespeople are paid on commission and can receive a bonus. Ms. Ocechuku can be a good manager if she is successful at getting the salespeople to meet their targets. In contrast, if Ms. Ocechuku has a vision of growing the market for the company's shoes and imparts this vision to the salespeople, so that she excites and inspires them, and they find new and innovative ways to promote the shoes and increase sales and they feel good about helping achieve the vision, then she would be described as a good leader, not just a good manager. Although a manager can be a leader, there are situations where good managers are not leaders.

## Theories of Leadership

Leadership theories have evolved from trait theories (1930–1950), behavioural theories (1950s–1960s), situational/contingency theories (1960s–1970s) and charismatic /transformational theories (1980s–1990s). Early research sought to identify traits that could be associated with effective leaders. These included physical traits such as height, attractiveness and so on, as well as psychological traits such as intelligence, emotional stability and so on. This research was inconclusive—no traits that could reliably predict a good leader. This is often referred to as the 'Great Man' theory and in the African context the leader as the 'Big Man'. Interestingly, the idea remains; for example, when Mandela was released from prison after 27 years, many people commented that 'he looked like a leader'. Mandela was certainly a leader, but it was more than his physical appearance, his traits, that made him one. It is possible that certain traits may be important in certain parts of the world.

In the mid-twentieth century, leadership research focused on style. Leadership styles were discussed as task or people/relational oriented. Herzberg's theory termed these X and Y. Theory X managers/leaders were task-oriented and believed employees did not want to work and worked only for economic benefits. They did not give employees responsibility and did not trust them; instead, employees were rewarded for good performance and disciplined for less than standard. Theory Y managers/leaders were people-oriented, believed people wanted to work and would respond positively to open communication, trust and responsibility. Theory Y managers/leaders believed that paying attention to employees would lead to satisfaction and high performance.

During the 1980s, Japanese companies had a prolonged period of success and American companies lost market share to them. Formerly, 'American management' had been the model of good management, but in the 1980s people became interested in Japanese management/leadership. Ouchi (1981) developed Theory Z based on comparisons of American and Japanese firms. Theory Z is largely people-oriented (using terms already discussed) but goes beyond theory Y. It seeks to increase loyalty through long-term job security and social interactions, and uses consensual decision-making (described as bottom up) and quality circles for improving group performance; evaluation and promotion procedures are slow, and theory Z believes employees should be generalists rather than specialists, using job rotation and constant training to increase knowledge of the company and its processes. Like theory Y, theory Z is based on the belief that employees want to work and can be trusted.

The literature has moved beyond the task–people/relations dichotomy, but some form of these two dimensions show up in leadership research around the world. In African countries, two styles have been discussed that fit this picture. The first is the powerful leader, who uses his place at the top of the hierarchy to accomplish objectives. The second is the communal, servant leader, who sees leadership as for the good of others and the community. Some argue that colonialism supported and contributed to the authoritarian, task-oriented leadership style, while the more traditional African style was communal. Ubuntu, for example, is often described as representing a communal approach to leadership (Malunga, 2009).

### Contingency Leadership

Leadership theories that followed task/people/relations approaches were called contingency theories, based on the idea that the best leadership style depended (were contingent) on the situation. That is, there is no 'best style' but aspects of the environment, and the nature of the leader/followers, determine effective leadership. The environment includes culture, laws and regulations, politics and so on. To be an effective leader in African countries, the environment has to be understood.

Contingency leadership initially considered the task–people/relations dichotomy and asked 'what situations suggest a task approach, and which a people approach?' For example, a task approach is appropriate when urgent action is needed (if there is a fire), where subordinates are inexperienced, or where superior–subordinate relationships are not friendly. A people approach is appropriate where time is available for developmental activities, subordinates are familiar with the task, and where superior–subordinate interactions are positive. Initially these theories proposed leadership styles as either task-oriented or people-oriented. Fiedler proposed that the situation could be analysed to determine the most appropriate style in a given situation—ranging from those where relationships between the manager and employees were good, the task was highly structured and the manager had a high degree of power or control to situations where manager–employee relations were poor, tasks not well defined and the manager had little power. At the extremes, a task-oriented manager was needed while in moderate situations, a relational manager would be most effective. Fiedler argued that managers were essentially either task or people-oriented and their style could be evaluated and matched to a given situation.

A refinement of contingency theories was that a leader could be both task and people-oriented and that an effective leader adapted her or his style depending on the situation. For example, new employees often want and require a task-oriented leader to help them succeed with their new job, over time, employees need less task guidance and more people orientation to help them fit in, understand the culture and develop relationships. Once employees are thoroughly familiar with the task, they want even more people orientation to help them develop, further their career and so on. Finally, employees who are well established, need little support and largely can be left on their own.

The task and people aspects of leadership seem to be relevant in all situations. According to Dorfman (2004) considerate, supportive leaders are preferred around the world, but reactions to task-orientation are more complex. Most people probably see a task orientation as relevant to business success, but how the task is explained and accepted likely varies because of factors such as culture. Dorfman suggested, for example, that where power differentials are accepted, a directive/task approach would probably work well. In societies where leaders/managers are believed to be in those positions because of their attributes (e.g. decision-making ability, expertise, social standing or a variety of other characteristics), they will be expected to make decisions, while lower level employees will expect to do what they are told. In these societies, attempts to delegate and involve employees in decision-making may actually be demotivating.

Many of the leadership theories that have been explored in more recent years are what we can describe as 'overarching' or 'big picture' and encompass many previous ideas. Three of these are Charismatic Leadership, Engaged Leadership and Transformational Leadership. We briefly discuss these.

### *Charismatic Leaders*

Charismatic leaders have an innate ability to attract followers who want to do what the leader wants. Charismatic leaders are eloquent in their communication, persuasive and the force of their personality attracts others. The GLOBE (Global Leadership and organisational Effectiveness) project (House et al., 2004) concluded that charismatic or value-based leadership was universally endorsed. This style was described as the ability to inspire, motivate and expect high performance from others based on core values. Other concepts associated with charisma were visionary, self-sacrifice, decisive and performance oriented. Visionary and inspirational leadership were also endorsed by African respondents in the LEAD research project.

While charisma in general is felt to be an effective style of leadership, it is also important that the actual behaviour of a charismatic leader may vary dramatically. Hitler is described as 'charismatic' and is almost universally believed to have been morally evil. Mandela is described as 'charismatic' and is almost universally believed to have been morally an exemplar. One challenge with the concept of charisma is whether it can in some sense be developed in leaders. To many people it seems more like an innate concept— that is, some people are charismatic and attract others to follow them, while others are not.

### Transformational Leaders

Transformational leadership is similar to charismatic and engaged leadership. A transformational leader works with teams to identify needed change, creates a shared vision to guide the change through inspiration and executes change together with committed members of a group. While the similarities to the other leadership styles are clear, the immediate focus of this leadership theory change—the leader is the catalyst that transforms the organisation. These leaders have the ability to get followers to go beyond the normal functioning of the organisation to transforming it and enabling it to reach new levels. A transformational leader gets followers to give up old ways of behaving, so change can take place and become the new normal. Clearly in the world situation of the coronavirus pandemic, there was great need for transformational leaders. Organisations and states were faced with a completely new situation that called for new ways of doing things. Those entities that reacted well in this situation did so because their leaders had the ability to identify needed change and guide the organisation through the difficult situation.

Transformational leaders enhance the motivation, morale and performance of followers by connecting their individual sense of identity with a project, and their collective identity with the organisation. They are role models for followers and inspire them; challenging followers to take greater ownership for their work, and understanding followers' strengths and weaknesses, which allows the leader to align followers with tasks that enhance performance. Transformational leaders are strong in the abilities to adapt to different situations, share a collective consciousness, self-manage and are inspirational while leading a group of employees. Transformational leaders are critical in times of change and particularly important for African organisations in today's changing world.

## *Engaged Leaders*

Engaged leadership is described as inclusive and stressing respect for others, including concern for development and well-being. Engaged leadership is related to servant leadership and characterised by the ability to unite different groups of stakeholders and articulate a shared vision through a developmental culture. It includes giving others responsibility and encouraging questioning and critical thinking to foster individuals' potential. Engaged leadership is based on integrity, openness, transparency and genuinely valuing the contributions of others. An engaged leader never asks someone to do something she or he would not do. A focus on people is apparent but engaged leaders also resolve complex problems and are decisive, enabling organisations to be proactive in dealing with change. An engaged leader combines a focus on people and task, as well as incorporating characteristics of a charismatic leader, such as being visionary.

Engaged leadership is particularly relevant for today's youth, and African countries have large young populations and need to find ways to engage them in the workplace. These countries are also facing substantial change as they grow and develop economically and socially, and become increasingly international; a situation exacerbated by the coronavirus pandemic of 2020. In facing change and turning it to advantage, engaged leadership can provide an edge. The LEAD study found that an effective leader in Africa is engaged, with the attributes of both a servant and transformational leader. These findings also suggest ethical leadership and behavioural attributes such as valuing people, building community, sharing leadership and qualities of honesty, fairness and concern for others as important attributes of effective leadership. While this style was preferred, the reality in African countries is often described as almost the reverse. This suggests a need for substantial training and development to reorient the thinking and behaviour of leaders to a more engaged style.

## *Toxic Leadership*

A negative style of leadership is destructive or toxic, with negative consequences for employees and the organisation, and to be avoided. Effective leadership engages in mutually agreed goals with followers working towards organisational objectives. On the contrary, destructive leadership influences others to obtain personal power, for his or her selfish goals/interests. Destructive/toxic leaders are described as having the following characteristics: abuse, tyranny, evil, callous, hostility, coercion, liar, incompetent, rigid, insular, theft, malice, harassment, bullying, unethical and ridiculing (Bice, 2020). Toxic leaders might be competent and effective in a short-sighted sense, but they contribute to an un-healthy work climate with ramifications extending beyond their tenure. These leaders show an apparent lack of concern for the well-being of subordinates or interpersonal techniques, and this negatively affects organisational climate. Along similar lines, the GLOBE study identified a Self-Protective leadership dimension consisting of sub-scales; self-protective, status conscious, conflict inducing, face-saving and procedural. This type of leadership was universally thought of as negative. Toxic leaders should be avoided in organisations, as their behaviour tends to lead to employee turnover, employee stress and lack of motivation. To protect against toxic leaders the following are recommended: good pre-employment screening processes, empowering employees against the influence of toxic leaders, generating an ethical organisational culture.

## The Meaning and Importance of Motivation

Organisations depend on the activities and behaviours of people who work there, and it is said 'people are the organisation's most valuable resource'. Even with automation, people are required, and motivation is a key aspect of management. Success and profitability are directly related to the performance and productivity of people; thus, a major component of a manager's role is ensuring that employees are performing at the best possible level.

We talk of people being highly motivated when they work hard to accomplish objectives that are consistent with the organisation's goals and talk of people being de-motivated when they seem disinterested and have to be pushed to perform. In both cases, we observe behaviour, but not the cause. Theories of motivation seek to identify the causes of behaviour. It is not really correct to talk of people being de-motivated; more likely they are motivated by something that is not related to work. We briefly examine the main theories of motivation proposed over the past century or so.

## Theories of Motivation

We consider the role of needs, equity, rewards, expectations, goals and delegation/participation. For simplicity, we discuss each separately, but they are interrelated. Broadly, theories of motivation may apply universally, but details can differ from location to location.

### *Need Theories*

These are based on the idea that people have certain needs, and their behaviours are designed to help fulfil those needs. People act in ways they believe will result in their needs being met. If someone is hungry (need) they will look for food. Behaviour reflects the need. This may be thought of as a universal relationship. What and how people seek for food may, however, differ from place to place. In some situations, one might look for a restaurant, while in others you might go out to the field and pick something to eat. Some people might want something like a hamburger, while vegetarians would consider that option unpleasant. Needs are often described in a hierarchy:

- Basic: the physiological level that deals with survival, food, water, shelter, sex.
- Security: assurance that basic needs will continue to be met.
- Social: interaction with others—friendship, relationships, communication.
- Esteem: feeling positive about oneself—praise, recognition, self-esteem.
- Higher level: self-actualisation—being the best one can be, doing what is important, accomplishing difficult goals.

Maslow proposed that each level becomes important, and a motivating force, once the previous level had been more or less satisfied. That is, the basic, physiological needs are paramount until satisfied. Once fulfilled, a person focuses on security, then on social and so on.

The levels of needs go from concrete to abstract as one moves from 1 to 5. At the survival level, needs can be clearly defined and likely apply to all people. At the highest, self-actualisation, needs are imprecise and vary from person to person. Self-actualisation could mean leading an ascetic and spiritual life or it could mean becoming very wealthy and important. At the lowest levels, needs are likely similar across countries and cultures; at the higher levels, they may be substantially influenced by country and culture differences. Even at the lowest level, however, what/when/how we eat and drink may depend on where we are. For example, the typical breakfast in much of China consists of soup and/or noodles, a breakfast that many North Americans find difficult to contemplate. Kenkey and fish might be considered normal breakfast food in parts of Ghana and a Ghanaian accustomed to this might not find a sweetened cereal with cow's milk (typical in North America) particularly attractive. Even within countries, eating habits may differ between the urban and rural populations, or among ethnic groups/tribes. One of the effects of globalisation is felt on eating habits where people are increasingly behaving in similar ways such as drinking coca cola.

Lower level needs are important to people everywhere. If people are hungry and have no shelter, meeting these needs will be most important, and little else will motivate them until these needs are met. The order of the other needs may vary. For example, in some cultures, individual self-actualisation may be frowned upon whereas communal accomplishments may be considered most important. The word ubuntu, used in reference to some African countries, and translated to 'I am because we are' has been described as the belief in a universal bond of sharing that connects all humanity. This implies that in societies that subscribe to Ubuntu, people are expected to prioritise community needs over individual needs.

There are other theories that incorporate needs as motivators. One that is often used in the organisational literature is McClelland's, which proposed a wide array of needs and argued that some were more important to some people, and that different needs would come to the fore in different situations. The needs usually considered in organisations are need for power, achievement and affiliation. People with a high need for power seek out important positions and enjoy using their power. People with a high need for achievement want to perform at a high level and feel good about what they do. People with a high need for affiliation enjoy being with others and want to work closely in teams and to be appreciated by team members.

The Herzberg model proposed two sets of factors associated with any job—intrinsic and extrinsic. Intrinsic factors are associated with the job itself; such as how interesting, varied, challenging and rewarding the work is. Extrinsic factors are not related to the job; things such as physical conditions, pay, benefits, supervision, co-workers and so on. Herzberg argued that extrinsic factors needed to be adequate for employees to be satisfied, but that it was the intrinsic factors that actually motivated. He believed that people worked hard and were productive when intrinsic factors were present. There is some cross-cultural research that suggests that this is true among better off people, but less true among people who are relatively poor.

One can argue that lower level needs and extrinsic job characteristics may be particularly relevant in poor countries and at lower levels in organisations. Given the relative poverty in many African countries, it may be that to motivate employees, the focus should be on ensuring that they receive adequate compensation and benefits to cover their basic needs. These employees may be motivated more by a safe working environment than the opportunity to learn new techniques (interest) or have a varied work schedule (variety). There is anecdotal evidence from one company in Africa that virtually eliminated absenteeism and increased productivity by providing breakfast for daily workers. This seems logical—if workers are poor and do not eat in the morning, they may not come to work because they are searching for food. If they do come to work, they may not be as productive because they lack nourishment. Providing breakfast is relatively inexpensive (perhaps bread, eggs, rice) and gives workers an incentive to get to work and then they are better able to perform well.

There is other anecdotal evidence from a group of low-level employees offered the opportunity to do their own quality checks (to increase responsibility and autonomy and variety of the jobs) who refused. They said they preferred to do the jobs they knew well, because this allowed them to talk with their friends (social). Asked why they enjoyed working at their company, they said it was because of the clean factory and the uniforms that were provided (extrinsic factors).

## Process Theories

Other theories of motivation involve equity, expectations, rewards and goals. All of these also incorporate needs, so we may think of them as going beyond simply looking at needs. If we understand someone's needs, we can better understand what is equitable, what expectations they have and so on. The following sections briefly explain these theories.

### Equity Theory

Equity theory was first proposed in the 1960s and refers to the fairness people perceive in a situation. Basically, individuals consider what they put into a situation and what they get out of it and compare the ratio of inputs to outcomes to some other(s) they consider comparable. To give an example:

> If a student works hard for a particular course, goes to classes and hands in all the assignments (these are her inputs) and ends up with a 'B' (her outcome), she will compare this input/outcome ratio to that of others in the class. If the ratio seems fair she will continue to be motivated to work hard. If on the other hand, others seem to have done little work but received a higher mark, the comparison will seem unfair. She may then believe that her inputs are not related to the outcomes, and reduce her inputs in future.

It is likely that people everywhere look for some sense of equity, but differences occur over what are seen as appropriate inputs/outcomes, and who one compares oneself to. In the student example, working hard for the course is the main input. Suppose she is in a society where males are always given higher marks than women, then being a woman becomes an input if she compares herself to all classmates. Alternatively, she would only compare herself to other women. Gender biases remain the case in a number of locations and may affect what is seen as equitable. This is certainly true in parts of Africa as elsewhere. It is also the case in parts of Africa, that ethnicity, tribal loyalty, political loyalty and status may convey a certain standing or prestige and affect what is seen as equitable. This is also the case elsewhere, for example, the President of the USA (2016–2020) reportedly fired people in his administration who were not loyal to him, even though they were professionally competent.

Equity theory stresses the importance of evaluating and rewarding people fairly, so that hard work and good performance are encouraged. This is the ideal that we propose. Nevertheless, we accept that there may be variations because of culture. In some societies, it may be that a person's need is considered relevant—a person with six children has a greater need than a single person and, in such a culture, rewarding the single person because of hard work might actually be seen as inequitable. The challenge for managers is to understand what constitutes inputs, what outcomes are valued and how comparisons are made.

*Expectancy Theory*

Expectancy theory was first proposed in the 1960s and is based on people's expectations about the outcome of their actions. It suggests that a person looks at a situation and asks: (1) If I try harder/put in a lot of effort, will my performance improve? (2) If my performance improves, will my rewards increase? (3) How much do I value these rewards? Think of the answers as varying from 0 to 1. If the answer is clearly 'no' the score is 0, if clearly 'yes', the score is 1. If in-between, then some fraction to indicate how close to no or yes. If the answer to any of the questions is no (0) then the person will not be motivated to put in much effort. In contrast, the higher the score (closer to 1) the more motivated the person will be.

This theory has implicit western biases. It is individual based, and assumes an individual can logically assess a situation in terms of relationships. It assumes that the individual has options and control over their environment. In many parts of the world, the context may be very different. The group may be more important than the individual, the workplace is controlled by those in positions of power, and logic is more circular than linear.

In the western/North American literature, expectancy theory illustrates the need to ensure employees feel they can perform well if they put in effort, understand their goals, rewards need to be allocated according to performance and rewards must be valued. Although there may be western bias in the theory, the lessons are appropriate elsewhere. Employees need to see a relationship between increased effort and performance, they need to see that increased effort/performance is rewarded, and the rewards need to be valued. These relationships hold in Africa as elsewhere. In the next section, we are going to look at the role of rewards in motivation.

*Reinforcement Theory*

Reinforcement theory of motivation is based on the work of B.F. Skinner and which drew on the earlier work of Pavlov with animal training. Reinforcement relates largely to the role of rewards in motivation and behaviour. Rewards seem to be inextricably bound with the concept of motivation. In terms of needs, when the inner urges are satisfied, whatever satisfies them is the reward. If we are hungry and find a nice mango on a nearby tree, the mango is the reward. In equity theory, we need to believe that the rewards are distributed fairly, and in expectancy theory, we consider how much we value rewards. The idea of rewards in the workplace is largely taken for granted today. If someone does a job they will be paid for it, usually with money, but sometimes 'in kind'. We often think first of money as a reward, and when we make arrangements for someone to do a job, the monetary aspects (pay, bonuses, benefits) are discussed explicitly. However, there are other rewards that are not as clear, such as a corner office, or a large one with mahogany furniture, and other so-called 'perks' (short for perquisite and meaning an advantage beyond one's pay) that may be desirable and seen as a reward for good performance. Rewards also go well beyond tangible expressions, and include praise, recognition, preferred assignments, acceptance by co-workers, personal time and so on.

Rewards are generally seen as a means to encourage desired behaviour, and withholding rewards as a way to discourage behaviour that is unwanted. This is known in the literature as Reinforcement theory. We use reinforcement in life all the time. Mothers (and fathers) will tell their children they can have ice cream (or some preferred treat) if they do their homework, and withhold the treat if the homework is not completed, dog trainers give dogs a treat when they obey a command and so on. In the workplace, a manager may give incentives to those who arrive at work on-time or deny privileges for those who are absent from work. Reinforcement is also, however, culturally contingent, in terms of the details; that is, what we use as rewards, when we give rewards and how we give them.

In North America, money is considered a valued reward and increased compensation is used to motivate employees who perform well. In other locations, people work until they have enough to pay for necessities, and additional money may mean that they stop working until they need more money. Generally, in Africa, the situation is similar to North America as people expect to be given more money when they perform well. In North America, it is considered appropriate to single out an individual for doing a good job. In other places, being singled out has negative connotations and rewards for group performance are more fitting. In Africa being singled out for having done a good job and being rewarded publicly is common; for example the Ibo people in Nigeria held traditional wrestling competitions and winners were named in public, given trophies and held in high esteem.

In North America coaching—where the positive aspects of work are highlighted and suggestions for improvement made—is considered a motivating approach. In other places, outright criticism is preferred and people want to be told when they have made mistakes. In the Africa context, people would usually not feel good to be berated in public as that is seen as not respectful. This is even more serious if the person criticising the other is younger than the one being criticised. One would therefore expect to be counselled or warned in private.

In addition, rewards can be given publicly or privately, they may be formal or informal, they can be given by superiors, co-workers or subordinates, they can be frequent or seldom, based on short-term performance or longer term, they may be small or substantial or sequentially graduated. All of these factors impact the effectiveness of rewards. In order to motivate employees, it is important to identify the kinds of rewards that are desirable, and to determine how and when to give rewards.

## Goal-Setting

There is substantial evidence that goals help people focus their energies and improve performance. The North American literature has linked specific and challenging goals, once they are accepted and linked to desired rewards, to increased outputs. Specific and difficult goals, on their own, significantly increase performance over 'do best' or no goals. Although difficult goals are desirable there is also evidence that goals need to be achievable. Thus, unreachable goals may actually be counter-productive. Some studies have linked participation in goal-setting to goal acceptance and thus to their effectiveness.

Studies of goals cross-nationally indicate that goals are effective under a wide array of national conditions. Based on this, we believe that goals may be effective in many circumstances; however, there may be societal and cultural conditions that affect the usefulness of goal-setting. For example, in communist countries where payments are set by the ruling party and increased performance does not result in increased rewards, goals may be less effective. In the PRC in the 1980s, referred to as the 'iron rice bowl', workers were often seen playing *mah jong* once they had completed the minimum tasks required. Certain cultural values might also interact with goals. Collective societies might prefer group goals; societies preferring certainty might see difficult goals as risky; societies high on power distance might prefer goals to be set by superiors; a very feminine might see goals as engendering competition and regard them negatively, and so on.

## Conclusion

The theories discussed here are intended to give the reader a grounding in well-accepted theories. These have been developed in the West, particularly the United States. In discussing leadership, we talked of contingency theories that illustrated the need to match leadership style to the environment. The same is true of motivation. To motivate employees to perform at an acceptable or better level, the societal and situational characteristics have to be taken into account.

## Review/Discussion

1. Select two leadership theories and compare and contrast them. Identify and explain which you think would be most appropriate in your country.
2. Select two motivational theories and compare and contrast them. Identify and explain which you think would be most appropriate in your country.
3. Discuss how leadership relates to motivation and why certain leadership styles would be more likely to motivate employees than others.
4. Given that Africa generally has a young population, explain what type of leader is likely to be effective.
5. Given that Africa generally has a young population, explain how what is likely to motivate them as employees.

## Exercise

Betty Jane Smith is a seasoned manager with many years' experience in her Australian mining firm. She has been asked to spend a couple of years at the Tanzania subsidiary. The Australian company is pleased with the performance at the subsidiary but believes the top managers will benefit from leadership development. Betty Jane had previously been involved with leadership development at headquarters and other subsidiaries in Latin America. She is looking forward to the opportunity. She has visited Tanzania on a number of occasions, as well as other African countries, both as a tourist and in a business capacity. She enjoyed those visits and made friends with locals and expatriates.

Knowing the cultural differences, she decides that on arrival in Tanzania she will initially meet with each manager individually in his office and ask how he thinks he personally can benefit from leadership development and solicit ideas bout helpful training programs. She plans to share her ideas with each manager to get their feedback, before deciding on the specifics of the program to implement. She emails the managers (Adulla, Bill and others) when upon getting to her hotel and asks them to suggest meeting times starting the following day.

### *Assignment*

1. Using the scenario described, identify aspects of the culture and context that will be important for Betty Jane Smith to consider as she proceeds with her assignment.
2. Based on the culture and context, discuss how successful you think her proposed approach will be.
3. Betty Jane wants to be an engaged leader and to ensure that all the top managers are also engaged leaders. Discuss how you would advise her to proceed with the management development program.

## References

Dorfman, P. W. (2004). Prior literature on performance. *Journal of Management*, 12, 83–90.

House, R. J., Hanges, P. J., Javidan, M., Dorfman, P. W., & Gupta, V. (2004). *Culture, Leadership and Organisations: The GLOBE Study of 62 Societies*. Thousand Oaks, CA: Sage Publications.

Malunga, C. W. (2009). *Understanding Organisational Leadership through Ubuntu*. London: Adonis & Abbey Publishers.

Ouchi, W. (1981). *Theory Z: How American Business Can Meet the Japanese Challenge*. Reading, MA: Addison-Wesley.

Punnett, B. J. (2019). *International Perspectives on Organizational Behavior*, 4th edition, New York: Routledge, Taylor and Francis.

# 7 Controlling

## Chapter Summary

The final management activity is controlling—measuring achievement, comparing it with established objectives/goals and taking corrective action where necessary to align actual results with agreed objectives/goals. Controlling is designed to help in assessing if the organisation is progressing as it intends towards agreed outcomes. Organisational controls take many forms; they can be formal or informal, loose, or tight, centralised or decentralised and so on. In this chapter, we also consider corporate governance as a particular form of controlling.

---

### Learning Outcomes

After completing this chapter, you will be able to:

- Define the concept of control.
- Describe the activities involved in controlling.
- Identify and explain different types of controls.
- Explain how to make controls effective.
- Identify and discuss aspects of the African context in terms of organisational controls.
- Relate the concept of corporate governance to controls.

---

## Definition

Controlling is the design and implementation of standards of performance that allow measurement of outcomes compared with standards. Control is pervasive at the individual level and in all forms organisation. In social organisations, control may be related to ensuring that individual behaviour conforms with group norms such as family expectations. Formal

DOI: 10.4324/9781003017516-7

organisations use controls to align individual behaviour with organisational norms, so that employee's actions are on the path to achieving objectives/ goals that lead in the desired strategic direction. Controlling and planning are closely related. Planning determines goals and strategies and the means to attain them, and controls measure progress towards attainment of goals. Effective controls identify deviations and their causes, and alert management when corrective action is needed. In the next sections we consider various aspects of control.

## Dimensions of Organisational Controls

Controls vary along several dimensions as follows:

- Formalisation: controls can be formal and specific, or they can be less formal and somewhat general. For example, 'employees are entitled to two-days sick leave per month, and must follow these steps in applying for sick leave' versus 'employees who are not well need to talk to their supervisor about the situation'.
- Centralisation: controls can be determined at headquarters and applied to all units in an organisation, or they can be decentralised, with different controls determined by individual units.
- Bureaucracy: controls can be detailed, written and applied rigorously in all situations, or they can be more personal and take the situation into consideration.
- Visualisation: controls can be seen and judged. In a small organisation, a manager can look around the office or factory floor and see if anyone is missing. If someone is missing the manager can take corrective action by talking to the missing employee. In small African companies much controlling is visual. This is more difficult as companies become larger.
- Procedures: step-by-step statements of how a particular activity is carried out. For example, washroom cleaners in restaurants may have a list: wash hands, mix ½ cup cleaner in 1 gallon water, clean basins . . . and so on; as each step is completed a tick is placed next to that item, and random checks are done to ensure the procedures are being followed. Procedural controls may be combined with visual ones.
- Embeddedness: Some controls are automatic. In an electronic assembly if wires are twisted incorrectly, there is a beep to alert the employee. These ensure that activities are performed correctly. Automatic saving of computer input is such a control. These may require sophisticated technology and may be more costly than other control approaches; thus, they are only applicable where the technology is available, useable and within cost constraints.

Continuing technology advancements experienced globally, and within Africa, mean that embedded controls are likely to become more common. For example, where lights come on and off automatically, or where a helpline is expected to greet the customer by saying 'Hello Mr. Taleb' (his name), if she or he does not, an artificial intelligence recorder, prompts this greeting. Generally, large organisations are more likely to have formal, centralised and bureaucratic controls, while small firms and family-owned ones are more likely to rely on informal, individually determined controls. This is true in African as elsewhere.

Overall, control systems will likely become more sophisticated and incorporate more technology in coming years. Nevertheless, controls that are visual and rely on procedures will remain part of the controls used in the everyday workplace. With the COVID-19 pandemic, more organisations have found that employees can work at home, remotely, rather than in an office. It is not possible to have visual controls in the usual sense, but it is possible to monitor employees remotely, through computer screens and so on. Some people feel this is invasive, but companies are using this as a control mechanism.

## Classifications

Organisational controls fall into three main levels. Macroscopic controls focus on the entire organisation and larger groups within it. These controls are accomplished through rules, policies and hierarchy and coordinating mechanisms. Administrative controls focus on departments within the organisations. Individual controls focus on individual behaviour. Controls cover a wide variety of activities and processes as presented below.

> *Budgetary*: Most organisational units have budgets for various activities, ranging from utilities to travel to supplies. They are expected to operate within these budgets and must justify any deviations or have additional expenses authorised. Actual expenditures and budgeted ones are reviewed to identify deviations and underlying causes and corrective actions.
>
> *Sales-related*: Most sales units have expectations regarding sales/revenues for various lines, departments, territories and so on, for particular time periods. The actual sales/revenues are reviewed regularly and compared to targets. Based on this information, in a subsequent planning season, targets may be revised appropriately or additional sales activities explored.
>
> *Production-related*: Most units have performance and production requirements. For example, in a helpline unit, operators may be

required to spend an average time on each call (say 5 minutes), to use specified phrases and greetings, and to offer additional products or services to callers. Calls are recorded and compared to the specified standards. Deviations may result in additional training, warnings, sanctions and so on.

*Policy-related:* Most units have manuals, which set out policies and procedures. These cover a range of expected behaviours and situations and specify the results of non-conformance. For example, the manual for a retail store might specify that sales clerks be at their stations 5 minutes before store opening, a visual inspection will be made, and if a clerk is not in position, she or he will be issued a verbal reminder and so on.

*Quality-related:* Many units have quality requirements, particularly where physical parts have to conform to legal or industry standards, and parts are tested against standards. Quality standards may also be set for services; for example, customer satisfaction may be judged through surveys and employees are required to score above a certain level.

## Characteristics of Effective Controls

Punnett and Ricks (1997) identified six important attributes of control systems:

### *Accuracy*

What is to be measured and how it is measured are critical elements of controls. If the objective is to have two day's stock of a certain part (say 1,000 widgets) in the warehouse, actual stocks must be checked regularly and if the inventory counts are accurate, this control will be effective. In contrast, if inventory counts are guesstimates (it looks like we have about the right amount), this may lead to negative consequences such as stock outs.

### *Timeliness*

Information is only useful if available in time to take corrective action or make necessary changes to goals/objectives or strategic direction. If information is late it can result in delays, if it is too early it can lead to inappropriate responses. Timing and speed of measurement and reporting are important. Decisions on when the object of control is measured and who responds are critical. In the widget example, should they be counted daily, every two days, randomly, and who is responsible for ordering when the count reaches a certain level, are decisions that need to be considered.

## *Objectivity*

Information, to the extent possible, should reflect observable facts rather than personal subjective opinions. In the case of the widget count, the guess based on simply looking at the boxes of widgets was not objective. Personal opinions may also be biased, and this should be taken into account where the type of information requires subjectivity. Controls based on objective measures are generally preferred to subjective ones and should be used wherever possible.

## *Acceptability*

Controls work only as well as the people who maintain them. If a system is unacceptable, members of an organisation may ignore it, sabotage it or comply with it unwillingly. As a result information is likely to be inaccurate, untimely and possibly subjective. An effective control system is therefore designed with the users in mind. In the case of the widgets, the person(s) responsible for keeping a count must see that it is important to do this and they must have the appropriate numerical skills.

## *Clarity*

Information is useful insofar as it is understandable and readily interpretable by those who use it. If it is unclear, it may be ignored, can be misunderstood and may lead to mistaken actions. In the case of widgets, a count of boxes combined with a visual inspection to confirm they are full is relatively simple and should be clear. In contrast, a more complex calculation relating to the number of current orders, previously completed orders, upcoming orders and so on, might be less clear, unless the employee has the necessary training.

## *Cost-Effectiveness*

A good control system provides greater benefits than the cost of designing, implementing and maintaining it. If the costs in terms of time and effort out-weigh the benefits, then there is no gain from the system. In the case of a widget count, if the system costs are relatively low and it is important to avoid a stock out, then the control is cost-effective. If it requires substantial time and effort, and there are readily available substitutes, then it may be unnecessary. Effective control systems need to be justified in terms of costs and benefits.

Each control system is distinct to the particular organisation, and units within it. There are generic control systems that can be purchased (e.g. accounting and financial systems, quality control, performance measures) but these need to be evaluated and modified in the context of the organisation's particular strategy, and goals/objectives. The system should be relevant to the organisation's unique characteristics and should be monitored to determine how well it performs. An effective system includes:

- Determining desired final results.
- Identifying interim results that will lead to desired final results.
- Establishing standards for final results.
- Collecting data and comparing with standards.
- Identifying causes of deviation.
- Taking corrective action.
- Comparing actual results with expectations.
- Reviewing plans and goals.

Organisations vary on many dimensions and pursue varying strategies, therefore the types of controls that are appropriate also vary. In the next section we consider some aspects of organisations that affect controls, particularly with a focus on the African context.

## The African Context

It may seem at first that controls are more important for larger, more formally structured companies. It is the case that larger companies are likely to have more complex and encompassing systems than their smaller counterparts. Think, however, of someone in rural Africa in the informal economy, who has a few stands where she or he sells vegetables and employs two or three people to run these stands. Control is vital in such a case, or the employees may give away some of the produce to friends, sell it for a lower price than required, take some home, pocket some of the money and so on. The owner of the stands needs to have an accurate count of the merchandise, and the revenue collection (cash) has to match the quantity of sales. Similarly, she or he will want to do spot checks to ensure that the stands are being 'manned' ('personnel') at all times, that the merchandise is properly displayed, and so on. These are all part of a control system. In Africa, where much of the economy revolves around these small, informal enterprises, these types of controls will be needed. They will be specific to the activities that affect the venture's success or failure.

There are many family-owned firms in Africa, and this presents a special issue in terms of controls. In these firms, it is usual that family members work in the firm, and it may be difficult to control them, but it may be particularly important. Consider a firm where the eldest son is given responsibility for financial aspects of the firm (as may be traditional in the family), then it is discovered that he has a gambling problem. The family has to find ways to have controls over finances, so the son cannot gamble with the firm's money. The control mechanism might be to have all transactions reviewed and signed by more than one family member. Family issues are complex because they go well beyond business interests and affect family relationships; thus, they have to be handled carefully.

Larger companies and organisations in African countries have controls, which are typically bureaucratic; there are systems of standardised rules, methods and verifiable procedures. These systems are similar to those found elsewhere around the world. At the same time, lower levels of education may require adaptation of these systems to ensure that they are effective with lower level employees, who may have relatively low literacy and numeracy skills. Multi-national companies operating in Africa need to pay attention to the kinds of controls that are effective in the African context. For example, controls that work in the People's Republic of China may not be appropriate in some African countries.

So far we have focused on controlling at a micro level. However, organisations are also controlled at a broader level; control extends to the entire organisation. This is generally termed corporate governance. We discuss corporate governance next and relate to the African context.

## Corporate Governance

Corporate governance has been defined in various ways. The OECD (2015, p. 9) describes corporate governance as 'a set of relationships between a company's management, its board, its shareholders and other stakeholders'. Corporate governance provides structure for setting objectives, the means to attain them and performance monitoring. Cadbury (1992) defined corporate governance as: systems and processes by which organisations are directed and controlled.

Debates about corporate governance failures are particularly related to control. Failure in this sphere means the organisation may not achieve its mandates. This is true in for-profit and not-for-profit, large and small companies, including non-governmental organisations, foundations and trusts. From a corporate entity point of view, governance provides investors with confidence that their investments will be used efficiently to generate returns. Organisations produce the goods/services we consume, provide employment and are a source of revenue to governments (taxes) implying the importance corporate governance.

The mechanisms of corporate governance operate inside the organisation (i.e. board of directors, shareholders and lenders—in some cases) and outside (i.e. legal systems, competitive markets for labour, products and capital). The board of directors is the most important mechanism. This mechanism ensures that decisions that have controlling effects on the organisation are made and approved for implementation. For example, if management needs to significantly reduce the number of employees to control costs, it must seek and obtain the approval of the board of directors before it can implement that decision. The board must approve decisions that have organisation-wide effects. The board of directors is also responsible for installing a framework for control within the organisation. The various controls discussed earlier are related to corporate governance, as they support the way an organization is controlled and directed. Following, we discuss the board's control activities.

## Control Activities of the Board of Directors

The control activities of the board are embedded in its three main functions. Figure 7.1 summarises the control functions of the board and their linkages. These functions are: approving organisational goals and strategy, setting policies and procedures to be followed in implementing the strategy, and monitoring and evaluating goals and strategy, policies and procedures and take corrective steps where necessary.

The first function is approving the organisational goals and strategy, and the strategic plan. A strategic plan is prepared by management and presented at a board meeting, for consideration and final approval (after inputs

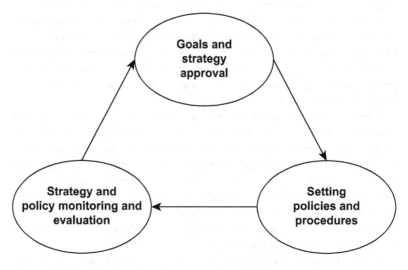

*Figure 7.1* Control-related functions of the Board of directors

or sacrifice them, but rather, ensure that while achieving one's interest, the interest of others should not be harmed. Behaving according to norms (rules of behaviour) of society, being ethical, may seem simple, but there are situations that present moral dilemmas. A moral dilemma arises when what is ethically right or wrong is not clear. A common dilemma in business in Africa is whether to give a bribe to win a contract and save an organisation or refuse to give a bribe, lose the contract and the organisation fails, leading to job and income losses for employees and their dependent families.

Both ethics and the law are meant to determine what is right in human interactions and society. Law is a standard of conduct, prescribed by the government for society to follow and is backed up by force, as actions against those who violate the law can be taken. Ethics is not backed by force and emanates from personal or community values. When ethics are codified into law, this reflects the values and norms of that specific society. Laws are expected to be fair and moral, but they are not necessarily founded on ethics. There can be unethical laws, such as the law allowing slave trade or apartheid laws. There are also laws where society is divided on their ethicality, such as laws on abortion or legalisation of same-sex marriages. Figure 8.1 shows relationships between virtues, values, ethics and law. At

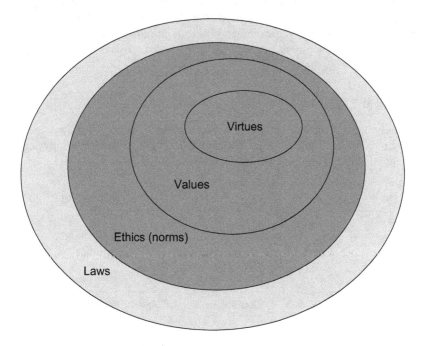

*Figure 8.1* Relationships between virtues, values, ethics and laws

the core of human behaviour are virtues; the next layer consists of values and society-endorsed values constitute ethics. Those deemed important should be enforced and constitute law.

To appreciate the difference between ethics and law, consider situations where following the law does not make an ethical person or when something ethical may not necessarily be lawful.

A company is located in a crowded suburb, with no proper drainage systems, and when it rains, water accumulates in low points and creates ponds leading to rampant malaria as mosquitos reproduce. People in this suburb throw litter around the ponds and this produces foul smell. Some company employees, especially unskilled ones, come from this neighbourhood. The company can fill the ponds and create a good neighbourhood or ignore it and focus on generating profit for shareholders. If the company chooses to fill the ponds, it is not because the law compels it, but rather the ethical values of the company (held by management) that inspire it to act this way.

There are also situations where ethics and the law conflict. Consider a situation where an accident has occurred; a driver of a private car stops to help the victims and takes the most seriously injured person to hospital. He goes through the red traffic lights—the action is ethically right but against the law. An action may be both unethical and illegal such as a student cheating in an examination or an employee stealing company property. Next we consider several theories that explain how one may decide what is ethical.

## Ethical Theories

These contain rules to determine if specific human actions can be judged right or wrong. Three theories are commonly used—virtue, deontology and consequential. Figure 8.2 portrays these in terms of their focus.

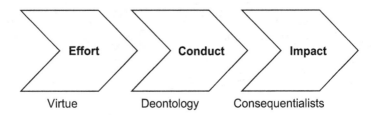

*Figure 8.2*  Three ethics theories

*Source*: Kaptein and Wempe (2002)

## *Virtue*

Virtue theory is traced to classical Greek thinkers, especially Aristotle (384–322 BCE), who synthesised Greek ideas to shape virtue theory. Virtues are acquired human qualities, the excellences of character, which enable a person to achieve the good life. Virtue theory focuses on what makes a good person not what makes a good action. A person may be ascribed various characteristics or attributes; usually not physical attributes such as beauty, age, height and size but abilities, intentions or motives. These latter qualities determine how an individual will act in morally demanding situations and can be evaluated in moral terms (Kaptein & Wempe, 2002). There are specific morally desirable traits that ethical persons must have, including civility, cooperativeness, courage, fairness, friendliness, generosity, honesty, justice, loyalty, self-confidence, self-control, modesty and tolerance. In business situations, virtue theory is usually applied through the promotion of desirable qualities by stipulating them in a code of conduct/ethics.

## *Deontology*

This theory is based on the actor's adherence to rules/principles. Deontology proposes that all persons have obligations, based on inalienable rights. An action is morally good if it honours a given obligation, irrespective of the consequence of the action. Deontological theory judges the morality of choices, the intentions or motives of actors by different criteria from the impact of those choices. Most people who subscribe to this theory agree that some choices cannot be justified by their effects—no matter how morally good the consequences, some choices are morally forbidden. For deontologists, what makes a choice right is its conformity with a moral norm. The motive for performing certain acts is to abide by a specific moral norm and never to achieve some good consequence. Deontological theory stipulates duties that must be observed, irrespective of their consequences: legitimate rights must be respected and unjust action is prohibited. The word 'deontological' comes from the Greek deon, 'one must' (Kaptein & Wempe, 2002). There are many variants of deontological theory including monism (Rose 1877–1971), Kantianism (Kant 1724–1804) and Justice (Rawl 1921–2002). The most common is Kantianism where human actions satisfy the categorical imperative, defined as a universal law or principle.

## *Consequential*

Consequentialism is based on outcomes of an action. The central idea is that actions are morally right if the consequences are desirable and bad/

wrong if they are not. It suggests a cost-benefit approach to the analysis of actions performed. People who apply this employ certain standards, purposes or ends, against which the consequences of an action are judged. This theory is subdivided into three sub-forms: egoism, utilitarianism and altruism (Kaptein & Wempe, 2002).

Egoism treats self-interest as the foundation of individual actions. An action is considered ethical if it produces good results for the person carrying out the action; that is, one should pursue his or her own interest. Egoism assumes each person should follow his or her own self-interest exclusively, and evaluate the ethicality of action in terms of the extent it promotes the interest of the self. If a sales supervisor denies opportunities for self-development to subordinates, fearing the staff will outshine him or her; the supervisor is applying ethical egoism.

Utilitarianism holds that the morally right action is the action that produces the most good for the majority. Actions are right if they affect everyone favourably resulting in maximum happiness to the greatest number of people. In business, the promotion of competition in the marketplace may be justified based on utilitarianism, that is, with more competition, buyers will get higher quality goods/services at lower prices.

Altruism believes an action is ethical if it produces good results for others. Altruism is associated with unselfish help to others and the ability to disregard one's own interests/desires. An altruistic self-sacrifice for the common good is always treated as ethical. If a company invests in programs to support environmental protection, this decision is based on ethical altruism.

## African Ethics

Gyekye (2010) considers African ethics as founded on humanism, considering human interests and welfare as basic to thought and action. In the African context, humanity is a moral term that is invoked when to considering relationships. What makes something good or bad, according to this standard is custom; that is, good is what receives community approval; bad is what is disapproved. Right builds society; wrong tears it down. This results in the communitarian ethos that the best way to ensure the welfare and interests of each member is through a focus on the community.

The African humanitarian ethics gives rise to social morality of the common good and morality of duty, including love, virtue and compassion. Relative to the theories discussed, African ethics considers actions as right if the consequences of such actions promote welfare of the society as whole—implying an altruistic utilitarian approach. Despite years of slave trade followed by colonialism, Africans have kept their values of community including ethical values, which probably developed early on during human evolution, when communities consisted of a hunter–gatherer economic system. Modernity, including education, may have lowered the intensity of these values but they still seem to be present. Research on culture has continued to find collectivist orientations among African societies.

Next, we discuss codes of conduct/ethics and how these relate to corporate social responsibility. These are tools for organisations to promote virtues, values and behaviours that are acceptable in those organisations.

## Codes of Conduct, Corporate Social Responsibility

The theories presented apply to business as they apply to other fields providing reference points when developing ethical values for organisational members and the organisation as a whole. Business ethics refers to organisational standards, principles or sets of values and norms that govern the actions and the behaviour of individuals in an organisation. In business the ethicality of economic activities depend on the interests of all involved in such activity. The virtues of organisations are manifested in the actions of its members. Business ethics are a set of moral rules, standards, codes or principles, providing guidelines for right behaviour in the business context. Managers develop ideas for ethical standards based on consideration of the theories outlined, although this usually happens without explicit reference to them. For example, the application of virtue theory is implicit in human resource policies formulated to encourage employees to develop certain attributes such as innovation. Consequentialist and deontological theories are reflected in the development of policies to deal with the environment, and other stakeholders.

We recognise that African culture is different from western culture and management theories (including ethics) developed in the west do not necessarily fit the African context. These theories are meant to apply in a context characterised by more individualistic tendencies compared to the African context. In the individualistic context, ethics have a different emphasis as the following illustrates.

> Jane and her family lived in a house in Barbados and had a second house on the same compound. Their friend from Africa moved to Barbados with his daughters and Jane and her family suggested they use the second house. Jane's family also owned a second car that they lent to their African friend. A couple of months later, Jane and her family wanted to sell their second car, Their African friend was hurt because he thought the car belonged to them all, that is, Jane's family as well as his. He thought of it as communal property.

This thinking can affect business situations and means that a manager should not take action that would disadvantage a colleague—especially a relative (e.g. firing if caught misusing company property) because that harms the colleague/relative's welfare. Communitarian thinking in business ethics emphasises community orientation over the individual. Theories created in individualistic cultures may not be appropriate in communal cultures; thus business ethics that work in the west may not work well in Africa. Business ethics relevant for Africa have to connect African ethical requirements to the objectives of business, which go beyond profit making. In Africa, a business would often be conceptualised as a social entity, with a role to consider community welfare. There is need to develop ethical theories consistent with African culture and Lutz (2009) suggests that when a firm is understood as a community, the purpose of management is neither to benefit individuals nor to benefit several collections of individuals as stakeholders, but to benefit the community and even larger communities of which it is a part.

The African community-oriented view has been referred to as Ubuntu philosophy. Desmond Tutu used the phrase '*umuntungumuntungabantu*', which means 'a person is a person through other persons' to describe this perspective. Tutu further emphasised the role of community in shaping individuals by stating that nobody comes into the world fully formed. Since businesses are creations of people, they need to be operated in ways that reproduce the ways of those who established them. Businesses should be seen as mechanisms that are created to serve people—customers, suppliers, lenders and the wider society. They should act as people normally would and keep the communal orientation in their business decisions/relationships. South Africa's Kings report defines organisational business ethics as 'ethical values applied to decision-making, conduct, and the relationship between the organisation, its stakeholders and the broader society' (Institute of Directors of South Africa, 2016, p. 12).

### *Codes of Conduct/Ethics*

A code of conduct/ethics is a statement of the ethical principles and values and behaviours expected of organisational members. They provide a mechanism for promoting ethical actions of the employees/members of the organisation. Codes of conduct/ethics are the foundations of religious traditions; for example, the Ten Commandments form the basis for beliefs in Judaism, Christianity and Islam (Gilman, 2005). Civic codes are also important; and Pericles, a Greek Emperor, promoted the Athenian Code as the foundation of ancient Greek politics and culture (Gilman 2005). Codes communicate general obligations and admonitions and provide a vision of excellence for which individuals and societies should strive. Similarly, business organisations have codes of conduct/ethics to help reach their goals.

Codes are usually written to guide behaviour or interactions with organisational stakeholders. Codes are designed to guide persons who want to act ethically, but codes, even if severely enforced, will make bad people good. There are three reasons why codes of ethics are prepared:

- When everyone knows the ethical standards, they can recognise wrongdoing and take corrective action.
- Even those with bad intentions will hesitate to commit an unethical act when everyone around them knows it is wrong.
- Corrupt individuals believe that they are more likely to get caught in environments that emphasise ethical behaviour.

Codes of ethics flow from the values of the organisation, contained in the guiding documents such as the vision, mission, values and strategic plan. For example, the strategic plan of the University of West Australia states: the University fosters the values of openness, honesty, tolerance, fairness and responsibility in social and moral, as well as academic matters. This is intended to assist staff and students to identify and resolve ethical issues that might arise during employment or studies. The code provides more specific information about the organisations policies, rules and expectations and includes: (1) the rights of employees to be treated fairly and equitably in the workplace; (2) avenues for resolving complaints or breaches of policies and codes and (3) the legal and ethical obligations and expectations of staff to act in accordance with the expressed standards of conduct, integrity and accountability, specified in relevant legislation, organisational policies and agreements.

### *Corporate Social Responsibility*

Corporate social responsibility (CSR) involves integrating social and environmental concerns into economic decisions of the organisation, to realise business objectives without harming the interests of stakeholders or others. CSR is justified using utilitarian or deontological arguments. Usually, the focus is the relationship between business and the environment, including all entities that affect or are affected by activities of business/corporation: for example, employees, suppliers, customers, financers, government and the community. Corporate citizenship and sustainability are two concepts associated with CSR. A common feature is a reflection of society's demands/

expectations. Corporate citizenship implies that corporations/organisations should behave like citizens and are required to follow the rules, laws and norms that apply in the country just like other citizens. Corporate sustainability implies that organisations need to undertake activities in ways that ensure they are sustainable and will continue to exist over a longer period of time.

There are many reasons why corporations should be concerned with CSR. Pressure from customers, suppliers and even investors has made companies consider social responsibility vital to their success. Based on the Cone Communications/Ebiquity Global study, some benefits of corporate social responsibility include improved organisational image, increased brand awareness and recognition, which give companies advantage over competitors, and enhance customer and employee engagement. Consumers are increasingly assessing organisations' public image in their buying decisions and news of an organisation's commitment to ethical practices will spread. For example, when employees volunteer for charities, it shows organisational commitment to helping others, and consumers are more favourable to the organisation. This is true for African companies—Tanzania Breweries Limited (TBL), a member of the Anheuser-Busch InBev group, manufactures, sells and distributes clear beer, alcoholic fruit beverages and non-alcoholic beverages says:

> Reputation is a key pillar that drives the way we do business and relate to the communities where we operate. Additionally, consumers consider more than just the quality of goods and services when choosing a brand, many are holding corporations accountable for effecting social change with their business practice and profits.

The following examples illustrate how companies in Africa view CSR:

### Dangote Cement

Dangote Industries Limited (https://dangote.com/), a Nigerian multination operates in 16 other African countries with turnover of about USD 4.1 billion in 2018. Its products include cement, sugar, salt, flour, pasta, beverages and real estate and it is expanding into the oil and gas, petrochemical, fertiliser and agricultural sectors. With respect to CSR, the 2018 Annual Report states:

> Strategic social investment is achieved through collaborative community projects based on our core themes of education, empowerment, employment and improvements in health.

Dangote has a Community Engagement Policy prioritising the establishment and nurturing of mutually beneficial relationships with host communities and emphasising the value their feedback. In 2018, the company reports the CSR activities including an investment of Nigerian Naira (₦) 1.4 billion of social investment for the construction of roads, schools, hospitals and several other public utilities to close some infrastructural gaps, and a fruit and vegetable processing training program specifically for women in Senegal, to help women from the Pout community to develop new skills.

## Tanga Cement

Tanga Cement in Tanzania was founded in 1980 as a state-owned company. Privatised in 1996, it is currently listed on the Dar es Salaam Stock Exchange. The company's Annual Report, 2018 states its CRS policy:

> We are committed to work with all our stakeholders, building and maintaining relations of mutual respect and trust. We aim to contribute and improve the quality of life of our workforce, their families and the communities around our operations. Our focus areas for social investments are health, education, community development and environment. The CSR policy statement is an important element of our business and serves as guidance for our decisions and actions. . . . Corporate Social Investment (CSI) policy is to invest up to 1% of profit before tax to specific and pre-defined projects, associations and charities.

> [. . .] During the year, the Group continued to support the Tanzanian society through its corporate social investment programs. . . . During the year, the Group contributed TZS 156 million (2017: TZS 91 million) towards various corporate social investment initiatives.

## Plasco Company Ltd

Plasco Company was founded in 1993 as a manufacturer of drinking straws. It steadily grew and currently manufactures high-quality plastic piping solutions for water supply, storage, sanitation, gas distribution and telecom networks using innovative world-class technology. Their vision is to become the leader for innovative water supply, storage and sanitation solutions in Africa. In their CSR Policy Statement, the company states:

> We are indebted to integrate social and environmental suitability. To reach such a milestone, we are committed to work with all our

stakeholders, building and maintaining relations of mutual respect and trust. We aim to contribute and improve the quality of life of our employees, their families and the communities around our operations. Our focus areas for social investments are access to clean water, sanitation, environmental and community development. . . . Corporate Social Responsibility policy is to invest up to 1% of its profit before tax to specific and pre- defined projects, associations and charities.

## Conclusion

In this chapter, we presented various aspects of business ethics. We described virtues, values, ethics and law and explained how these concepts are related. Three broad ethical theories were presented: virtue, deontological and consequentialist theories, as well as African ethics. We discussed business ethics in general, codes of ethics and codes of conduct and corporate social responsibility. The overriding is that businesses ethics apply in the context of business organisations just as they apply to other social and economic activities. Finally, we briefly discussed the humanistic approach to ethics to provide the context for decisions are made and implemented in the African context.

## Review/Discussion

1. Define and discuss what we mean by the term business ethics.
2. Values, ethics and the law are related concepts. Explain how they are related.
3. African ethics is described as being communitarian. Do you agree? Discuss.
4. Briefly explain the ethics theories presented.
5. Using examples, explain how ethics theories may be applied to justify business practices such as CSR.

## Exercise

### *The Businessman's Stay in a Hotel*

Abdul Mohammed is a prominent car dealer based in Mamboleo, in North–South. He also owns a number of hotels in East Africa and wants to expand to Tomo. Business in Mamboleo is seen as most profitable because of government subsidies that are available to attract foreign investments. Mr Mohammed has three potential partners to consider, and he makes a trip to North–South to meet with each of them. One of the potential partners, Mr Kiir, suggests that Mr Mohammed stay at his company's all-inclusive hotel while visiting and that he bring his family as the visit takes place during the school vacation. Mr Mohammed accepts the generous offer and he and family spend an enjoyable week at the all-inclusive hotel. Mr Mohammed reviews potential partners, and concludes that Mr Kirr is ideal. He enjoyed meeting Mr Kiir and his family socially, and feels they will be able to work well together.

*Assignment*

*Do you see any harm in this situation?*

### Case 2: Giving Gifts to Customs Officials

An importer based at Dar es Salaam has developed a good relationship with officials from the Tanzania Port Authority (TPA). This has proven helpful when she needs to clear items through customs. The officials will often put aside what they are doing to assist clearing her shipments. She maintains the friendship and says 'thank you' by taking the officials out for meals from time to time, and sometimes gives them small gifts at holidays.

*Assignment*

Do you see any *harm in this situation?*

## References

Gilman, S. C. (2005). Ethics codes and codes of conduct as tools for promoting an ethical and professional public service: Comparative successes and lessons. Prepared for the *PREM*. The World Bank, Washington, DC.

Gyekye, K. (2010). *African ethics*. Retrieved from https://plato.stanford.edu/entries/african-ethics/#TerEthMor.

Institute of Directors of South Africa, (2016). King IV Report on Corporate Governance for South Africa, http://www.iodsa.co.za, accessed 23 April, 2020.

Kaptein, M., & Wempe, J. (2002). *Three general theories of ethics and the integrative role of integrity theory*. Retrieved from file:///Users/melyoki/Downloads/017 ThreegeneralTheoriesofEthicsandtheIntegrativeRoleofIntegrityTheoryTBC-SSRN.pdf.

Lutz, D. (2009). African Ubuntu philosophy and global management. *Journal of Business Ethics*, 84, 313–328; Springer 2009.

Rokeach, M. (1973). *The Nature of Human Values*. New York, NY: Free Press.

Tuulik, K., Õunapuu, T., Kuimet, K., & Titov, E. (2016). Rokeach's instrumental and terminal values as descriptors of modern organisation values. *International Journal of Organisational Leadership*, 5, 151–161.

# Index

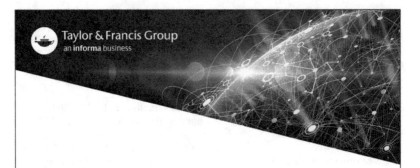